THE FORTRESS CHURCH

"Built for The Glory of God"

MICHAEL SCANTLEBURY

Books By Michael Scantlebury

Called to Be An Apostle – An Autobiography

Leaven Revealed

"I Will Build My Church." – Jesus Christ

Five Pillars of The Apostolic

Apostolic Purity

Apostolic Reformation

Internal Reformation

Jesus Christ The Apostle and High Priest of Our Profession

Kingdom Advancing Prayer – Volume I

Kingdom Advancing Prayer – Volume II

Kingdom Advancing Prayer – Volume III

God's Nature Expressed Through His Names

Identifying and Defeating The Jezebel Spirit

Available from Publishers: Word Alive Press wordalivepress.ca

About The Cover

The picture on the front cover depicts the Church of Jesus Christ, as atop the Mountain of the Lord and also as The Gate of Heaven. This Church functions both in Heaven and on earth. As one views the cover, we would like to bring to ones mind the following passages of Scripture:

> "Many peoples will come and say, "Come, let us go up to the mountain of the LORD, to the temple of the God of Jacob. He will teach us his ways, so that we may walk in his paths." The law will go out from Zion, the word of the LORD from Jerusalem." Isaiah 2:2-3

> "When Jacob awoke from his sleep, he thought, "Surely the LORD is in this place, and I was not aware of it." [17] He was afraid and said, "How awesome is this place! This is none other than the house of God; this is the gate of heaven." Genesis 28:16-17

> "Great is the LORD, and most worthy of praise, in the city of our God, his holy mountain. [2] Beautiful in its loftiness, the joy of the whole earth, like the heights of Zaphon is Mount Zion, the city of the Great King. [3] God is in her citadels; he has shown himself to be her fortress." Psalms 48:1-3

This Fortress Church causes Heaven's Will to be done in the earth. Whatsoever things we bind on earth would be bound in Heaven and whatsoever things we loose on earth would be loosed in Heaven!

This is the Church that Jesus said He would build!

Michael Scantlebury has taken author's prerogative in capitalizing certain words that are not usually capitalized according to standard grammatical practice. Also, please note that the name satan and related names are not capitalized as we choose not to acknowledge him, even to the point of disregarding standard grammatical practice.

All Scripture quotations, unless otherwise indicated, are taken from the New King James Version. All Scriptures marked RSV are taken from the Revised Standard Version, copyright © 1946, 1952, 1971 by the Division of Christian Education of the National Council of the Churches of Christ in the USA, and is used by permission. All Scriptures marked KJV are taken from the King James Version; all marked TLB are from The Living Bible; all marked AMP are from The Amplified Bible; those marked MSG are from The Message Bible; all marked GNB are taken from the Good News Bible; all marked ISV are taken from The International Standard Version and is used by permission. All Scriptures marked NIV are from the New International Version; Copyright © 1982 by Thomas Nelson, Inc. Used by permission. All rights reserved

Hebrew and Greek definitions are from James Strong, Strong's Exhaustive Concordance of the Bible (Peabody, MA: Hendrickson Publishers, n.d.).

The Fortress Church
ISBN 978-1-77069-586-3
All rights reserved: © Copyright 2012 – Michael Scantlebury

Published by: Word Alive Press – wordalivepress.ca
Printed in Canada.

Editorial Consultant: Anita Thompson – 604-521-6042
Cover design by: Michelle Soon – 604-789-9746

Library and Archives Canada Cataloguing in Publication
Scantlebury, Michael, 1958-
The fortress church / Michael Scantlebury.
ISBN 978-1-77069-586-3
    1. Church--Apostolicity. 2. Church renewal.
      i. Title.
      ii. BV601.2.S32 2012   262'.72   C2012-903116-X

A Mighty Fortress Is Our God
Martin Luther 1529/1528

1. A mighty fortress is our God, a bulwark never failing; our helper He amid the flood of mortal ills prevailing. For still our ancient foe doth seek to work us woe; his craft and power are great, and armed with cruel hate, on earth is not his equal.

2. Did we in our own strength confide, our striving would be losing, were not the right man on our side, the man of God's own choosing. Dost ask who that may be? Christ Jesus, it is He; Lord Sabaoth, His name, from age to age the same, and He must win the battle.

3. And though this world, with devils filled, should threaten to undo us, we will not fear, for God hath willed his truth to triumph through us. The prince of darkness grim, we tremble not for him; his rage we can endure, for lo, his doom is sure; one little word shall fell him.

4. That word above all earthly powers, no thanks to them, abideth; the Spirit and the gifts are ours, thru Him who with us sideth. Let goods and kindred go, this mortal life also; the body they may kill; God's truth abideth still; His Kingdom is forever. Martin Luther: 1483-1546

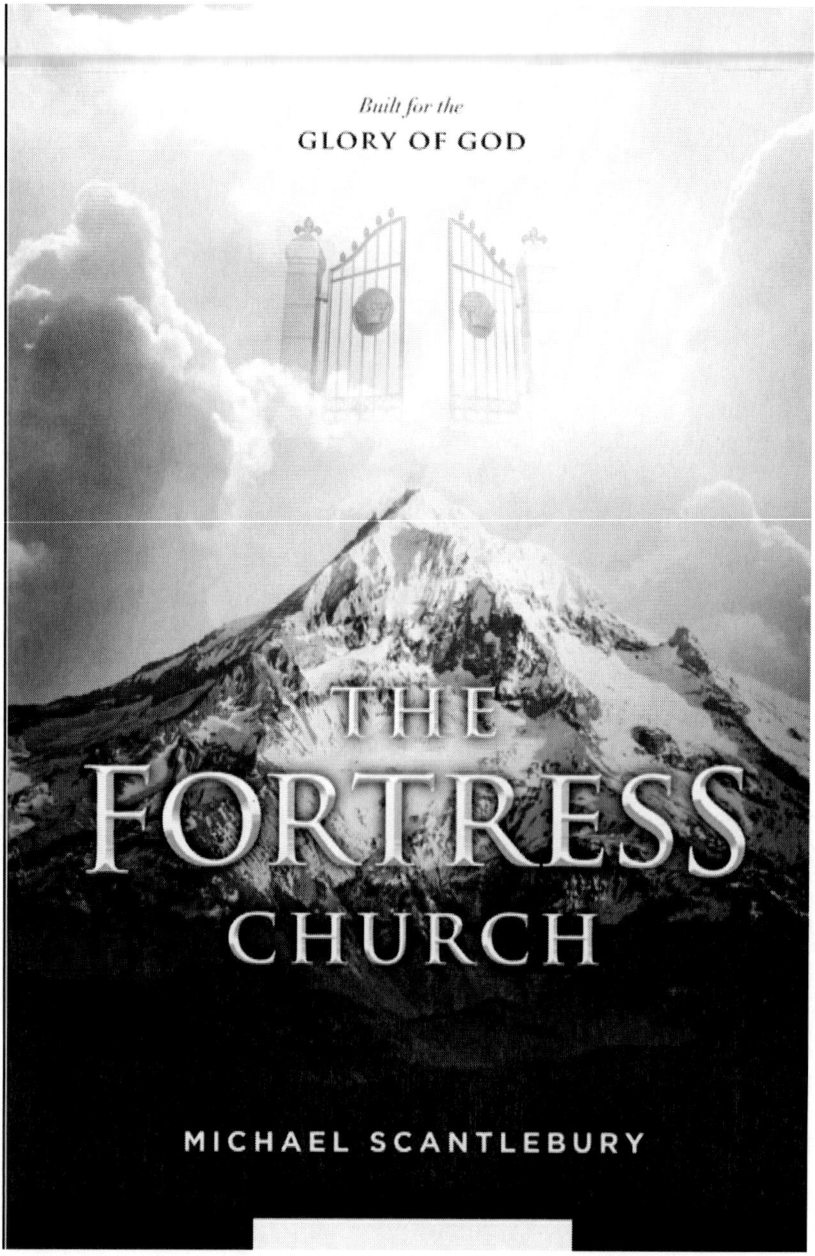

Built for the
GLORY OF GOD

THE FORTRESS CHURCH

MICHAEL SCANTLEBURY

Endorsements

The "Fortress Church" by Apostle Michael Scantlebury, is a catalyst for transformational change from deep within the foundation of the mindsets of leaders and followers of the Church of Jesus Christ. Transformed mindsets will result in the restructuring of the operational dynamics of the Church to make it the imposing change agent in the affairs of this world that God originally intended. Here is where this book really comes into its own both as a blue print for the new structure and a manual that will instruct and guide the builders according to the heart, will and purpose of God. I, therefore, endorse this book and recommend it as a 'must read' and 'must implement' for all leaders and congregations of the Fortress Church that God is building in these times of reformation.

Apostle Emmanuel Vivian Duncan
Divine Destiny Worship Centre
Diego Martin, Trinidad and Tobago

"Michael Scantlebury is a clear and concise writer with a tremendous gift of research in the true spirit of revelation. His other books have blessed many and The Fortress Church will continue this tradition. This book is highly needed for our day turning the minds of church leaders from the "Pop Culture" that are being used today to draw more people to a biblical mandate of a certain kind of church that is vitally needed. We must have a revelation of the Church that Jesus is building and I believe The Fortress Church will provide us insight into the mind and heart of the Lord for this day!"

Randy Boyd
Executive Director, Prepare International
Co-author – The Antioch Church Training Series

"This is a must read for anyone looking for present truth. The compassion and revelation that is given will be life changing. Understanding what God is trying to release in this hour to the Church is the key to opening new arenas of anointing. The truths contained in this book can destroy the darkness as we Believers and Leaders embrace the light of Christ to empower the invasion of Heaven in the Earth. These are truly Apostolic Strategies for our time. Thank you Apostle for being faithful to your calling and having an open ear to what God is releasing to our generation!"

Dr. BA Cook
The Leaders Edge, Inc
1305 Maxwell ST.
Salisbury, NC 28144

The Fortress Church is a people that not only know their identity but also operate in their identity. Michael brilliantly brings forth revelational truth in the Heavenly standards God has set forth for His Kingdom, and for His Fortress church. Ambassadors of His eternal Kingdom, living in the ordinances of heaven on earth, will be empowered to lead the gates of society towards radical transformation. If you want to go beyond religion and into the promises of God, this book gives you the scriptural blue print for the destiny for which you have been born.

Robert Ricciardelli
Founder Converging Zone Network
www.convergingzone.com

In every generation, God anoints men and women to skillfully articulate through writing, what He is doing in the earth. Their writings provoke, inspire, challenge and provide revelation for us to follow Christ more maturely. My friend, Apostle Michael Scantlebury, has just such grace from God. The Fortress Church, powerfully declares the arrival and building of an ascending governmental church. A strong, accurate, unified and mature church, the nations are coming to for God's wisdom. I highly recommend this resource for all saints and leaders called to work together to "build" churches impacting cities, regions and nations for the King and His Kingdom.

Apostle Daryl O'Neil
Ruach Covenant Church International

"The Fortress Church" by Apostle Michael Scantlebury is a forceful and impacting revelation of what the Church is "supposed to be."

What makes this book totally distinctive is that it will engage your determination to be a part of the answer. It provokes the "new breed" of what Apostle Michael calls the "true and proven Apostles" to rally toward the common focus of establishing this "Fortress Church"—one that is relevant in this day. A church that is potent, influential, and filled with Divine strategy.

While reading "Fortress Church," you will sense the mighty strength of God emerging through Apostle Michael's scholarship as he brings great awareness to the revolutionary changes that must happen in the Church, NOW!

Surely, "Fortress Church" convinces us that it's time for the [grown-up] sons of God to arise with intentional purpose to finish the mission that Jesus died to bring forth—and to fully establish His Church.

Read this book and join the revolution!

Dr. Kluane Spake
http://kluane.com
Commissioned Ambassadorial Apostle
President Jubilee Alliance Apostolic Network

What kind of Church does God need in the earth today to powerfully impact the nations for Christ and advance His Kingdom in this century? I believe this is one of the most important questions that Apostles and Prophets must answer. Apostle Michael Scantlebury is a visionary apostolic leader and gifted communicator whose new book "The Fortress Church" contains a revelatory exposition from Scripture that gives us an accurate and compelling picture of what this Church should look like.

As Michael Scantlebury's writing sketches for us from God's Word the blueprint of this powerful Church of influence, he also puts an emphasis on the profound truth that only through apostolic revelation can it be clearly seen, and only by apostolic wisdom can it be accurately built. The incredible supernatural design, architecture and dynamics of this glorious Church God has destined for planet earth is clearly found throughout Scripture. But because of centuries of tradition, much of the pattern of how to build it has been hidden from our spiritual eyes. The past 500 years of reformation ignited by Martin Luther and many others, have progressively brought the Church out of the dark ages, restoring to Her so many biblical truths that began to make Her strong and vibrant again.

Apostle Michael Scantlebury takes his place as a missional thinker, risk-taking pioneer and apostolic reformer in this 21st Century, who's published works concerning present truth, the restoration of the ministry gift of the Apostle, and the Apostolic Church, is making a tremendous contribution and impact to a fresh and new apostolic reformation movement that is circling the globe in this season and growing exponentially. I am pleased to endorse "The Fortress Church" as a must read for every ministry leader who desires a greater perspective and insight into the plan of God for His Church in this generation, and in the ones to come, and I want to commend Michael Scantlebury for giving us such a timely work.

Apostle Axel Sippach
Executive Director, IMPACT Network – impactnetwork.net

Table Of Contents

PREFACE — 013

CHAPTER 01: Dynamics of the Fortress Church I — 019
- Jacob's Vision — 019
- Gate of Heaven — 021
- The True Seed of Abraham — 035
- Principle & Promise of Unity — 041
- Focus — 053

CHAPTER 02: Dynamics of the Fortress Church II — 067
- The Psalmist View – Psalms 48 — 067
- In Jesus' Name — 070
- Return of the Elijah Spirit — 078

CHAPTER 03: Prophet Isaiah's Vision — 099
- The Blacksmiths — 102
- Destroying Babylon — 104

CHAPTER 04: The Antioch Church Model — 115
- Breakthrough Believers — 119

CHAPTER 05: From Blessing to Building Model — 137
- Apostolic Vision of the Church — 137
- Solomon's Temple – The Prototype — 138

CHAPTER 06:	The Church at Ephesus	163
	God's Ecclesia	166
	The Body of Christ	168
	God's Masterpiece	172
	The Family of God	174
	The Temple of God	179
	The Bride of Jesus Christ	183
	The Army of God	190

OTHER EXCITING TITLES BY AUTHOR   207

Preface

When we think of the word "fortress" images of castles housing kings, nobles and perhaps a few rogues come to mind, but also the mind's eye sees a massive structure situated in a strategic place and designed to defend. The medieval era during which many a fortress was built was a period of violence with sieges and assaults. The fortress had to withstand the attack of the enemy but it was also the centre of social activity for the surrounding villagers.

With this in mind the architecture of the fortress was designed to withstand great assaults by incorporating defence strategies such as a deep moat [a body of water surrounding the fortress], which with the help of a drawbridge could keep the enemy out, or be lowered to welcome guests to a feast.

The Lord has been talking to me for a long time about local churches across the earth representing Him. And in His wisdom, He has defined these local churches across the earth as "*Fortress churches*", Believers in Christ strategically placed for battle, and for reaching out to those in need, regaling them with the good news of the Gospel of the Kingdom.

According to Webster's English Dictionary "fortress" is defined as: a fortified place: stronghold, *especially*: A large and permanent fortification sometimes including a town. A place that is protected against attack!

In Scripture there are a number of words representing the various elements and aspects of the fortress. Here are a few:

1. Mibhtsar is the term generally rendered "fenced" or "defenced city." In both the King James Version and the Revised Version [British and American] of Isaiah and Jeremiah we find for the most part the more formal "defenced city." It is found by itself [Isaiah 17:3]; with `ir, "city" [1 Samuel 6:18; 2 Kings 3:19; plural `are mibhtsar, "fenced [the American Standard Revised Version "fortified"] cities," Numbers 32:17]; with tsor, "Tyre" [Joshua 19:29; 2 Samuel 24:7, where it is rendered "stronghold."]

2. Misgabh, "high fort" [Isaiah 25:12; Jeremiah 48:1 the Revised Version, margin; Psalms 9:9, and many other places in the Psalms.]

3. Ma`oz, "fortress," "stronghold" [Judges 6:26; Psalms 31:2; Daniel 11:39.]

4. Birah, "palace" the King James Version, "castle" the Revised Version [British and American] [Nehemiah 2:8; 7:2]. Birah Graecized is baris, which has the double meaning of "palace" and "fortress." Nehemiah's "castle" figures largely in the books of Maccabees and in Josephus, and is the Castle of Antonia of the Acts of the Apostles.

5. Ochuroma [2 Corinthians 10:4, its only occurrence in the New Testament though it is the chief equivalent of mibhtsar in the Septuagint]. In this connection it is to be noted that chomah, is Hebrew for "wall," Greek teichos; chel or cheyl, is Hebrew for the "ditch," or "rampart," or "bastion" of a fortress; mighdal, "tower"; pinnah plural pinnoth, "corner towers."

These are powerful words describing a building with an unshakeable foundation, a city high on a hill, a tower, prepared to defend.

However, before we go into the depths of what He has been speaking to me in defining the Fortress church, I would like to share one of the foundational elements or principles of such churches. I believe that this is very pivotal to the successful functioning of any local church regardless to where it is located across the earth. This is what is going to be referred to as "Divine Order."

Please understand that everything that God has created is built on "Divine Order." As we look at the natural order the birds and butterflies fly, the sun shines, day and night appear without effort. There is freedom as life flows. However, beneath all of what we see, beneath all that freedom is "Divine Order." In essence there is foundation and structure invisibly lying beneath all that manifest freedom. The Book of Job gives us irrefutable proof of this! Here are just a few examples as recorded in Job Chapter 38:

> "THEN THE Lord answered Job out of the whirlwind and said, ²Who is this that darkens counsel by words without knowledge? ³Gird up now your loins like a man, and I will demand of you, and you declare to Me. ⁴Where were you when I laid the foundation of the earth? Declare to Me, if you have and know understanding. ⁵Who determined the measures of the earth, if you know? Or who stretched the measuring line upon it? ⁶Upon what were the foundations of it fastened, or who laid its cornerstone, ⁷When the morning stars sang together and all the sons of God shouted for joy? ⁸Or who shut up the sea with doors when it broke forth and issued out of the womb?-- ⁹When I made the clouds the garment of it, and thick darkness a swaddling band for it, ¹⁰And marked for it My appointed boundary and set bars and doors, ¹¹And said, Thus far shall

you come and no farther; and here shall your proud waves be stayed? ¹²Have you commanded the morning since your days began and caused the dawn to know its place, ¹³So that [light] may get hold of the corners of the earth and shake the wickedness [of night] out of it? ¹⁴It is changed like clay into which a seal is pressed; and things stand out like a many-coloured garment. ¹⁵From the wicked their light is withheld, and their uplifted arm is broken. ¹⁶Have you explored the springs of the sea? Or have you walked in the recesses of the deep? ¹⁷Have the gates of death been revealed to you? Or have you seen the doors of deep darkness? ¹⁸Have you comprehended the breadth of the earth? Tell Me, if you know it all. ¹⁹Where is the way where light dwells? And as for darkness, where is its abode, ²⁰That you may conduct it to its home, and may know the paths to its house? ²¹You must know, since you were born then! Or because you are so extremely old! ²²Have you entered the treasuries of the snow, or have you seen the treasuries of the hail, ²³Which I have reserved for the time of trouble, for the day of battle and war? ²⁴By what way is the light distributed, or the east wind spread over the earth? ²⁵Who has prepared a channel for the torrents of rain, or a path for the thunderbolt, ²⁶To cause it to rain on the uninhabited land [and] on the desert where no man lives, ²⁷To satisfy the waste and desolate ground and to cause the tender grass to spring forth? ²⁸Has the rain a father? Or who has begotten the drops of dew? ²⁹Out of whose womb came the ice? And the hoary frost of heaven, who has given it birth? ³⁰The waters are congealed like stone, and the face of the deep is frozen. ³¹Can you bind the chains of [the cluster of stars called] Pleiades, or loose the cords of [the constellation] Orion? ³²Can you lead forth the signs of the zodiac in their season? Or can you guide [the stars of] the Bear with her young? ³³Do you know the ordinances of the heavens? Can you establish their rule upon the earth? ³⁴Can you lift up your voice to the clouds, so that an abundance of waters may cover you? ³⁵Can you send lightnings, that they may go and say to you, Here we are? ³⁶Who has put wisdom in the inward parts [or in the dark clouds]? Or who has given understanding to the mind [or to the meteor]? ³⁷Who can number the clouds by wisdom? Or who can pour out the [water] bottles of the heavens ³⁸When [heat has caused] the dust to run into a mass and the clods to cleave fast together? ³⁹Can you [Job] hunt the prey for the lion? Or satisfy the appetite of the young lions ⁴⁰When they couch in their dens or lie in wait in their hiding place? ⁴¹Who provides for the raven its prey when its young ones cry to God and wander about for lack of food?" [AMP]

Kingdom Life is a deliberate lifestyle. Things must be built according to plan. Jesus had disciples who He taught to walk a particular way. They understood that *freedom* had *foundation*.

Jesus was truly free, in fact He was the "freest" man upon the face of the earth and He did nothing apart from what He saw His Father do. In like manner I believe that every local church must have that *"Invisible Presence"* called *"Divine Order"* [the communion with the Father in doing His Will at all times] needed to operate, as we conduct our lives.

Into the next few pages I will be describing for you the "Fortress Church". I will be looking at the dynamics of this Church as described in Jacob's vision in Genesis Chapter 28, also as described by the Prophet Isaiah, in Isaiah Chapter 2.

It is also highlighted in a Psalm of the sons of Korah in Psalms Chapter 48. We also will look at a working model of this type of church as found at Antioch in the Book of Acts.

Finally we would be exploring the church at Ephesus, where the Apostle Paul by the Holy Spirit revealed some powerful descriptions of the Church, which can best be described as *"The Fortress Church"*!

☞ CHAPTER 1

DYNAMICS OF THE FORTRESS CHURCH I

Jacob's Vision!
A Description of a Strong, Governmental, *"Fortress Church!"*

Genesis 28:10-22

"Now Jacob went out from Beersheba and went toward Haran. 11 So he came to a certain place and stayed there all night, because the sun had set. And he took one of the stones of that place and put it at his head, and he lay down in that place to sleep. 12 Then he dreamed, and behold, a ladder *was* set up on the earth, and its top reached to heaven; and there the angels of God were ascending and descending on it. 13 And behold, the LORD stood above it and said: "I *am* the LORD God of Abraham your father and the God of Isaac; the land on which you lie I will give to you and your descendants. 14 Also your descendants shall be as the dust of the earth; you shall spread abroad to the west and the east, to the north and the south; and in you and in your seed all the families of the earth shall be blessed. 15 Behold, I *am* with you and will keep you wherever you go, and will bring you back to this land; for I will not leave you until I have done what I have spoken to you." 16 Then Jacob awoke from his sleep and said, "Surely the LORD is in this place, and I did not know *it.*" 17 And he was afraid and said, *"How awesome is this place! This is none other than the house of God, and this is the gate of heaven!"* ¹⁸ *Then Jacob rose early in the morning, and took the stone that he had put at his head, set it up as a pillar, and poured oil on top of it.* ¹⁹ *And he called the name of that place Bethel; but the name of that city had been Luz previously.* ²⁰ *Then Jacob made a vow, saying, "If God will be with me, and keep me in this way that I am going, and give me bread to eat and clothing to put on,* ²¹ *so that I come back to my father's house in peace, then the LORD shall be my God.* ²² *And this stone which I have set as a pillar shall be God's house, and of all that You give me I will surely give a tenth to You."* [Italics Added]

In this passage of Scripture, Jacob describes what he saw as nothing else but the House of God [verse 17] and identifies at least eight different characteristics about It.

- It is the GATE of Heaven – Verse 17!
- It has a very strong FOCUS – Causing the families of the earth to be blessed – Verse 14!
- It has many RESOURCES or resource personnel – Verse 13-14!
- It is a GIVING Church – The families are to be blessed through this Church – Verse 14!
- It is a VISIBLE Church – Angels are ascending and descending from It – Verse 12!
- It has a STRONG IMPACT upon the spirit realm – Verse 12!
- It would eventually IMPACT, the politics, economics and lifestyle of a nation – Verse 14!
- It has what we call a GOVERNMENTAL anointing – Verse 14!

The GATE of Heaven:
Gate: a point of entry! In essence then, the Church is an aperture or opening to the Heavens. From this we can deduce that God uses the local church that understands and operates as a gate or point of entry to Heaven to impact the earth: This is what I like to call a *"Fortress Church!"*

In Scripture, gates were always identified as places of authority and government. For example:

Deuteronomy 22:13-15
"If any man takes a wife, and goes in to her, and detests her, 14 and charges her with shameful conduct, and brings a bad name on her, and says, 'I took this woman, and when I came to her I found she *was* not a virgin,' 15 then the father and mother of the young woman shall take and bring out *the evidence of* the young woman's virginity to the elders of the city at the gate."

Deuteronomy 25:5-7
"If brothers dwell together, and one of them dies and has no son, the widow of the dead man shall not be *married* to a stranger outside *the family;* her husband's brother shall go in to her, take her as his wife, and perform the duty of a husband's brother to her. 6 And it shall be *that* the firstborn son which she bears will succeed to the name of his dead brother, that his name may not be blotted out of Israel. 7 But if the man does not want to take his brother's wife, then let his brother's wife go up to the gate to the elders, and say, 'My husband's brother refuses to raise up a name to his brother in Israel; he will not perform the duty of my husband's brother.'"

Psalms 24:7-10

"Lift up your heads, O you gates! And be lifted up, you everlasting doors! And the King of glory shall come in. ⁸ Who *is* this King of glory? The LORD strong and mighty, The LORD mighty in battle. ⁹ Lift up your heads, O you gates! Lift up, you everlasting doors! And the King of glory shall come in. ¹⁰ Who is this King of glory? The LORD of hosts, He *is* the King of glory. Selah"

Psalms 87:1-3

"His foundation *is* in the holy mountains. ² The LORD loves the gates of Zion More than all the dwellings of Jacob. ³ Glorious things are spoken of you, O city of God! Selah"

Psalms 100

"Make a joyful shout to the LORD, all you lands! ² Serve the LORD with gladness; Come before His presence with singing. ³ Know that the LORD, He *is* God; *It is* He *who* has made us, and not we ourselves; *We are* His people and the sheep of His pasture. ⁴ Enter into His gates with thanksgiving, *And* into His courts with praise. Be thankful to Him, *and* bless His name. ⁵ For the LORD *is* good; His mercy *is* everlasting, And His truth *endures* to all generations."

Proverbs 8:34

"Blessed is the man who listens to me, Watching daily at my gates, Waiting at the posts of my doors."

Proverbs 31:23, 31

"Her husband is known in the gates, When he sits among the elders of the land. ³¹ Give her of the fruit of her hands, And let her own works praise her in the gates."

Jesus admonishes us to enter in at a particular gate Matthew 7:13-14 and Luke 13:24

> "Enter by the narrow gate; for wide *is* the gate and broad *is* the way that leads to destruction, and there are many who go in by it. ¹⁴ Because narrow *is* the gate and difficult *is* the way which leads to life, and there are few who find it."
>
> "Strive to enter through the narrow gate, for many, I say to you, will seek to enter and will not be able."

The question now becomes: How do we construct this GATE of Heaven?

Let me offer at least seven things that are needed to do this. Of course I am sure that there are probably more:

- By The Strength And Purity Of Our Worship!
- By Bringing Our Hearts Into Unity!
- By Walking In Present Truth!
- By Receiving Revelation From The Lord!
- By Moving Accurately Into God's Purposes!
- By Allowing The Lord To Come Strongly Into Our Midst And Manifest Himself!
- By Constantly Changing Into The Image And Likeness Of Jesus!

By The Strength And Purity Of Our Worship.
The Scriptures declare that God inhabits or dwells in the Praises of His People.

Understanding The Power of Corporate Praise and Worship!

It is always good to remind ourselves about the reason why we must worship God and how important and powerful praise is. We need to be purposeful in heart as to why and how we worship, why it is an integral part of the Believer's life, and why in our assembly as a house we lift our hands, open our mouths and release our praise unto God.

There are several Hebrew and Greek words that translate Praise such as:
- Tehillah, "psalm," "praise!"
- Halal: "to praise, celebrate, glory, sing [praise], boast!"
- Todhah: "confession" "thanksgiving!"
- Shabhach: "to praise" "glorify!"
- Zamar, Yadhah: "to stretch out the hand," "confess!"
- Doxa: "glory," by "praise!"

There are several Hebrew and Greek words that translate Worship such as:
- Shachah: "to bow down", "to prostrate oneself before another in order to do Him honour and reverence!"
- Proskuneo: "kiss the hand in token of reverence", to kneel or prostrate to do homage!"
- Latreno: "to serve", "to offer gifts, to worship God!"

We will now take a look at Psalms Chapter 149 and draw some nuggets of truth out of it.

> "Praise the LORD! Sing to the LORD a new song, *And* His praise in the assembly of saints. ² Let Israel rejoice in their Maker; Let the children of Zion be joyful in their King. ³ Let them praise His name with the dance; Let them sing praises to Him with the

> timbrel and harp. ⁴ For the LORD takes pleasure in His people; He will beautify the humble with salvation. ⁵ Let the saints be joyful in glory; Let them sing aloud on their beds. ⁶ *Let* the high praises of God *be* in their mouth, And a two-edged sword in their hand, ⁷ To execute vengeance on the nations, And punishments on the peoples; ⁸ To bind their kings with chains, And their nobles with fetters of iron; ⁹ To execute on them the written judgment—This honour have all His saints. Praise the LORD!"

Psalms 149:1 says, "*Praise the Lord!*" and that's in the command form. The Psalmist is not saying, "*...maybe you should praise the Lord...*" or "*...Could I please, perhaps suggest that it might be fitting to praise the Lord.*" This is in the command form, "*Praise the Lord! Sing to the Lord a new song.*"

When the music is playing, the Saints are praising and we lift our hands and express ourselves before God, creating songs as we listen to the music and singing in a melody, using any words we please. Those are dimensions of the new song spoken of as well. So it's wonderful to *sing to the Lord*. Not only speak but also *sing* to Him.

"*Hallelujah*" and things that we would normally say, become songs sung unto the Lord in a very spontaneous way. The words "*new song*", suggests something spontaneous, something birthed of the spirit that springs right out of your inside as you lift up your hands. I would like you to underline the word *spontaneous* in your mind. It means that in this kind of worship you cannot say, "*...Well I'm just worshipping God in my heart*", or, "*I'm just enjoying the presence of the Saints.*"

It is participatory, it's effusive and it is spilling out of you. All of those concepts are contained in "*singing a new song*".

The line "*Sing His Praise In The Assembly Of The Saints*", means we're talking about corporate worship not individual praise and worship at home where you can sit quietly and sometimes muse upon God and get your box of Paper Napkins out and drop a tear or two and sniff [and some of you do that right?] It's healthy! It's wonderful!

Sit before God and just be overwhelmed by his intimacy! There are times when we worship God that way too. Every believer ought to know the intimacy of God. But it's tough to really get into the depths of that in a corporate worship service. When you're home, however, sometimes you find a nice quiet spot and you muse about God, His goodness, how wonderful He is what He has done for you. A little tear drops here and there and you get your Kleenex out... but you understand what I'm talking about, right? Worship in the privacy of your home is needed and necessary, but the Saints are admonished to do so in "*the assembly of the Saints*", when we come together. Emphasis on the word "*assembly*!" There is a praise that is "*In The Assembly Of The Saints*".

The word "assembly" in the Hebrew means: "The coming together part to part and piece to piece," like that of an intricate jigsaw puzzle where interlocking pieces fit perfectly.

I heard a preacher state that you can buy a bike in a box, but it doesn't work until you take out the instructions and assemble it. You see when you assemble the bike it becomes something that operates, that works, that is effective and useful. Similarly, you can have saints at work and at work you are a saint but there is something that is unique when we assemble, greet each other, say, I love you, and begin to sing together. That's what we are after!

Psalms 149:2 declare: "Let Israel [*Read The Church*] Rejoice In Their Maker And Let The Children Of Zion Be Joyful."

Emphasis is on the word "*joyful*", not face-dipped-in-lemon-juice sour. This means smile upon your face, eyes sparkling and not the eyes "dull and preoccupied", thinking about something else. That means every part of you activated dynamic, joyful, enthusiastic, enjoying being before God, worshipping him.

Verse 2 continues: "*Let Them Be Joyful In The King, Let Them Praise Him In The Dance.*" That means it's okay to shift from one foot to the other. It's all right to dance; it's all right to lift your hands, all right to give a hop and a jump. It's all right to make a movement and dance before the Lord and to give a little hop-skip and whatever. And it's all right to be out of sync and off key. God doesn't care. Some of you have a little problem keeping to the beat, who cares? Rejoice off the beat if you like. It is all right to dance and release yourself. That means that your body enters into praise. It means that your physical being expresses the enthusiasm and joy of your worship unto God.

Verse 3 states: "*Let Them Sing Praises To Him With The Timbrel And Harp!*" If this Psalm were being written today it would say, "...with the electronic keyboard, the drums and computers. Some people say, "...well you can only use the tambourine and a guitar." Come on, please. One man decided that harp spoken of in the Bible means only stringed instruments so you can be sure that God doesn't like drums and drums should not be used! So some churches don't have drums because of that person's interpretation and it is nonsense! Those were the only instruments David and the musicians of his time had, so in our day you can use the full range: you can use whatever you need from the vast array of musical instruments available to mankind, as well as spoons, sticks, oil drums [steel drum], etc.

Verse 4a states: "*For The Lord Takes Pleasure In His People...*" Underline in you mind: *takes pleasure*. The context is of a people that are worshipping God and God actually loves it.

He takes pleasure and you could write in what is unstated "*He takes pleasure in His people who are praising Him*". So when we are praising, God is actually taking pleasure, enjoying it, as He is receiving something. It must be unique and wonderful to make an eternal spirit receive joy. There is something in our worship that is absolutely unique.

"*God takes pleasure in his people and he will* beautify *the humble with salvation!*" I want you to understand the processes that are taking place: as we worship God He begins to take pleasure and He begins to beautify, [*the word beautify means "to adorn, to embellish, to give favour, divine grace."*] God's response is that He puts something on us that makes us better than we were before. That word "salvation" does not mean that He will get you saved; remember that you are already saved. But rather it is speaking of all of the benefits and the powers and the resources and the out flows of the grace of salvation will begin to be imparted to your life by God in the midst of your praise. Hallelujah!

Remember the Bible says, "*praise with understanding*". You are supposed to praise with understanding, not ignorance. When you praise with understanding you are aware that as you praise and worship God among the saints there are dynamic things that are happening that you can receive and you must be aware of. One of the things you must be aware of is that God is taking pleasure and that's your key to praising him with real enthusiasm. The other thing you should be aware of is that upon the individual who praises, God will begin to beautify, adorn, embellish with divine favour, with all of the benefits of salvation. Praisers are blessed people and I expect to get some beautifying when I am praising God and lifting him up. I expect all of the great resources of my salvation to be activated in my life. Breakthroughs and the security of God, the love of God, the sense of progressive impact in the things of the Kingdom must come upon my life and make me better. *Remember He didn't 'uglify' you with salvation; He beautified you.* We all know that salvation is to go from one level to the other. It is progressive.

Verses 5-6 proclaim: "*Let The Saints Be Joyful In Glory, Let Them Sing Aloud Upon Their Beds. Let The High Praises Be In Their Mouths*!" That does not mean you must shout Hallelujah at four in the morning and wake up all your neighbours [although you can.] It simply means that this worship is not only contained within the context of an ordered service, but is talking about a lifestyle. Praise and worship must spill out of the corporate context into your lifestyle. What we receive when we come together in the atmosphere of praise and worship must be taken into our individual lifestyle and must be expressed.

"*Sing Aloud Upon Their Beds, Let The High Praises Be In Their Hearts? No, No*! Let the high praises be in their *Mouths*. It must be vocal and expressed. High praises must not be kept in the heart. There is nowhere in the bible saying that high praises should be kept in your heart. High praise is always expressed vocally. It is an expression of the mouth; your ears must hear what your mouth is saying. Let the high praises be in your mouth means there has to be strong vocal expression.

Notice it is not the low praise; it is the *high praise* in your mouth and the two edged sword in your hand... What is the two edged sword? The Word of God is our sword. It means in worship you can speak the Word or you can praise God with things that you have seen in the Word. Its all right to say, "Worthy is the Lamb," you saw it in Revelation. It is all right to say "blessing and majesty, dominion and power be unto Him", you read it in the Bible. It's all right to say, "Bless the Lord, O my soul and everything that is in me bless His Name".

His Word in praise gives the praise sharpness, strength, power and penetration in the realm of the spirit. Expressing that which the Word says with understanding through your lips makes your praise more effective. If you read some of the Psalms you can get some good stuff from David that he used to say that you could express before God just to make a declaration of whom God is. These Words can be reiterated in your praise so that the high praises of God is in your mouth.

To do what? Verse 7 clearly answers that: *"Praise Executes Vengeance On The Nations."* So, not only does God receive pleasure when we praise Him, not only does He relate to your individual life by beautifying the humble with salvation, but your praise also has an impact globally. So what is done on a Sunday morning or at any worship service, feeds into the Purpose of God in the nations.

I see it like this: could you imagine churches all over the world are praising God and it goes up like a river and joins a mighty river, like tributaries joining. And all the praises go together in one gush and that gush accomplishes *the plan of God*. Not your church or ministry, but the plans and purpose for the nations.

So corporate praise must be heard in the earth because God says that praise is released – *"To Execute Vengeance On The Nations And Punishments On The Peoples"*. That is the purpose of God being released into a sinful earth. It is the praise of God's people that is like lubrication that makes God's purpose slide forward without hindrance. It is very important that when we come together, our voice must be heard.

Note also in Verse 8 *That It Binds Their Kings With Chains.* [These kings refer to demonic kings in the heavenlies] and their princes with iron handcuffs. Not only does our praise give God pleasure, bless our own life, join to the global purpose of God in the earth but it also explodes into the spirit realm and binds the devil up. Notice – they do not speak of little devils, but underworld kings. These are the powerful spirits that lie unseen behind the movements and strategies of Satan in the earth. The kings and princes are bound, jailed, handcuffed, resisted, restrained, hindered; their strategies are broken up because of the praise that is going forth into the earth. So when we say, "Blessing and honour, glory and power unto You the Mighty God" something explodes in the spirit and shuts a devil up. I like that! We have that great authority from the word of God. I want everybody to understand this, when we have corporate praise and you lift your hands and shout Hallelujah you are taking part in a great, mighty warfare. Remember Jehoshaphat in 2 Chronicles Chapter 20 and also Saul and David in 1 Samuel Chapter 14!

God coordinated it as He took this stuff from everywhere. Jesus is *the* Leader of *The Church*. We all know that there is One Church in the earth, all kinds of little groups, but One Church and it has one Senior Leader who is Jesus and we are brothers and sisters. There is no such thing as "well our little independent" or "my little denomination". No such thing! We are all One Church and we must insist upon that. There is One Global Church. It's The Only Church of Jesus. The Senior Pastor is Jesus; Co-Pastor: The Holy Ghost; Governing Authority: The Father; and then all of us.

When we lift our hands up and begin to worship it hits the devil and begins to bind his kings with chains and his princes of darkness with iron handcuffs. It has executive power to destroy governing things that the devil wants to do. Things that are being birthed in secret and his counsels are disrupted because of the praise of the Saints.

"It executes upon them, that is the demonic kings and nobles, the written judgments of God." God has these things "highlighted and underlined" in His "master computer" saying, – for example: I will destroy the devils over Vancouver in 2012 and He wrote that since the beginning of time! Written judgments, plans that are inscribed in the Heart and Mind of God to be unleashed upon the enemy are released through the praise of the Saints. I hope you understand how important this is!!!

Here is what I tell the Saints whom I have the honour and privilege to lead in building a *"Fortress Church"* unto the Lord: Brethren we need to come here in the morning and lift our hands with full enthusiasm, smiling faces, dancing feet, new songs in our mouth vocalizing the things of God, filling the place with expressions of praise with understanding. And as we do God will use them to do battle in the heavenlies against His and our foes! He uses us as His weapons of war, as His Battleaxes [will expound on this in more details in chapter three]!

Now I like the last line of Psalms 149: *"This Honour Have ALL The Saints."* It is indeed an honour and a privilege. "This Honour," to come into the Assembly of the Saints, lift your hands up and worship God. Everybody should be involved in it. I want us to understand what we are doing when we come together. As we lift our hands and worship we are bringing to pass the will of God in the earth!

Hebrews 13:15 "Therefore by Him let us [the people] offer the *sacrifice of praise*..." That means our praise is a sacrifice, not like the Old Testament. Our worship is a sacrifice to God that when we come in and start to lift our hands to God it is an offering to Him. Quite apart from getting beautified giving Him pleasure beating up those devils, joining the river, releasing into the nations, we are also offering up unto God a sacrifice. And in case we didn't understand what the sacrifice is it says, "...*that is the fruit of our lips*" It is the fruit of our LIPS, and not understandings in the heart. I want to focus on that "*fruit*" and what I am saying is that fruit comes when the tree is mature hence fruit comes from fullness.

Praise is the fruit of your lips it is the best of your speaking, the ripeness of your utterance. It is not quietly saying, "Praise God." Fruit is speaking with understanding and expressions before God. It's called the sacrifice of praise the fruit of our lips – Hebrews 13:15

Is it in the New Testament? Yes it is. Is it for today's church? Yes it is. And is God pleased with it? Oh yes, He is well pleased!

Just remember Saints... when we are praising we are called to praise and worship God, to bless God, to be beautified with salvation, to progress in the things of God.

However, we need to also understand that as we construct these places of worship across the earth, known as *"Gateway or Fortress Churches"* that the devil also has his gates or places of authority! In Matthew 16:18-19 Jesus Christ declares:

> "And I also say to you that you are Peter, and on this rock I will build My church, and the gates of Hades shall not prevail against it. [19] And I will give you the keys of the kingdom of heaven, and whatever you bind on earth will be bound in heaven, and whatever you loose on earth will be loosed in heaven."

As a *Fortress Church* we have the power and authority to dismantle and destroy the gates of the enemy. In doing so we will set the captives free and bring glory to the King of kings and Lord of lords, our King, Jesus Christ!

Genesis 22:14-18 and Genesis 24:51-60 *presents two very vital and key Scriptures:*

> "And Abraham called the name of the place, The-LORD-Will-Provide; as it is said *to* this day, "In the Mount of the LORD it shall be provided." [15] Then the Angel of the LORD called to Abraham a second time out of heaven, [16] and said: "By Myself I have sworn, says the LORD, because you have done this thing, and have not withheld your son, your only *son*— [17] blessing I will bless you, and multiplying I will multiply your descendants as the stars of the heaven and as the sand which *is* on the seashore; and your descendants shall possess the gate of their enemies. [18] In your seed all the nations of the earth shall be blessed, because you have obeyed My voice." [Genesis 22:14-18]

> "Here *is* Rebekah before you; take *her* and go, and let her be your master's son's wife, as the LORD has spoken." [52] And it came to pass, when Abraham's servant heard their words, that he worshiped the LORD, *bowing himself* to the earth. [53] Then the servant brought out jewellery of silver, jewellery of gold, and clothing, and gave *them* to Rebekah. He also gave precious things to her brother and to her mother. [54] And he and the men who *were* with him ate and drank and stayed all night. Then they arose in the morning, and he said, "Send me away to my master." [55] But her brother and her mother said, "Let the young woman

stay with us *a few* days, at least ten; after that she may go." ⁵⁶ And he said to them, "Do not hinder me, since the LORD has prospered my way; send me away so that I may go to my master." ⁵⁷ So they said, "We will call the young woman and ask her personally." ⁵⁸ Then they called Rebekah and said to her, "Will you go with this man?" And she said, "I will go." ⁵⁹ So they sent away Rebekah their sister and her nurse, and Abraham's servant and his men. ⁶⁰ And they blessed Rebekah and said to her: "Our sister, *may* you *become The mother of* thousands of ten thousands; And may your descendants possess The gates of those who hate them." [Genesis 24:51-60]

We, the *Fortress Church* are being raised up by God to take away the authority from demonic elders and establish the rule of the Kingdom of God in their place! Daniel 7:13-14, 27 also reveal this:

"I was watching in the night visions, And behold, *One* like the Son of Man, Coming with the clouds of heaven! He came to the Ancient of Days, And they brought Him near before Him. ¹⁴ Then to Him was given dominion and glory and a kingdom, That all peoples, nations, and languages should serve Him. His dominion *is* an everlasting dominion, Which shall not pass away, And His kingdom *the one* Which shall not be destroyed.²⁷ Then the kingdom and dominion, And the greatness of the kingdoms under the whole heaven, Shall be given to the people, the saints of the Most High. His kingdom *is* an everlasting kingdom, And all dominions shall serve and obey Him."

The Scriptures Teach Us That We, The Church Of Jesus Christ Are The True Seed Of Abraham – Galatians 3:6-18

"Just as Abraham *"believed God, and it was accounted to him for righteousness."* [7] Therefore know that only those who are of faith are sons of Abraham. [8] And the Scripture, foreseeing that God would justify the Gentiles by faith, preached the gospel to Abraham beforehand, *saying, "In you all the nations shall be blessed."* [9] So then those who *are* of faith are blessed with believing Abraham. [10] For as many as are of the works of the law are under the curse; for it is written, *"Cursed is everyone who does not continue in all things which are written in the book of the law, to do them."* [11] But that no one is justified by the law in the sight of God *is* evident, for *"the just shall live by faith."* [12] Yet the law is not of faith, but *"the man who does them shall live by them."* [13] Christ has redeemed us from the curse of the law, having become a curse for us [for it is written, *"Cursed is everyone who hangs on a tree"*], [14] that the blessing of Abraham might come upon the Gentiles in Christ Jesus, that we might receive the promise of the Spirit through faith. [15] Brethren, I speak in the manner of men: Though *it is* only a man's covenant, yet *if it is* confirmed, no one annuls or adds to it. [16] Now to Abraham and his Seed were the promises made. He does not say, "And to seeds," as of many, but as of one, *"And to your Seed,"* who is Christ. [17] And this I say, *that* the law, which was four hundred and thirty years later, cannot annul the covenant that was confirmed before by God in Christ, that it should make the promise of no effect. [18] For if the inheritance *is* of the law, *it is* no longer of promise; but God gave *it* to Abraham by promise."

As the Church of Jesus Christ, we will rule in those gates for we have been destined to do so, this is true government.

By Bringing Our Hearts Into Unity!
The second thing that we need to do is to make sure that we flow in unity. This is vital because in order for the Lord to truly move in His Governmental Authority there must be unity.

In John Chapter 17, Jesus expressed the fact that He had completed the work that the Father sent Him to do. Consequently, He was aware that His final moments on the earth were at hand. He therefore offered an intercessory prayer for those who must continue His work in the earth. In so doing, much of the mind of Christ in relation to this world and His Church is revealed to us. Let us take this opportunity to review some of the issues that were on Christ's mind at this time.

John 17:1-23 NIV
> "¹After Jesus said this, He looked toward heaven and prayed: "Father, the time has come. Glorify your Son, that Your Son may glorify You. ²For You granted Him authority over all people that He might give eternal life to all those You have given Him. ³Now this is eternal life: that they may know You, the only true God, and Jesus Christ, whom You have sent. ⁴I have brought You glory on earth by completing the work You gave Me to do. ⁵And now, Father, glorify Me in Your presence with the glory I had with You before the world began ⁶"I have revealed You to those whom You gave me out of the world. They were Yours; You gave them to Me and they have obeyed Your word. ⁷Now they know that everything You have given Me comes from You. ⁸For I gave them the words You gave Me and they accepted them. They knew with certainty that I came from You, and they believed that You sent Me. ⁹I pray for them. I am not praying for the world, but for those You have given Me, for they are

Yours. ¹⁰All I have is Yours, and all You have is Mine. And glory has come to Me through them. ¹¹I will remain in the world no longer, but they are still in the world, and I am coming to You. Holy Father, protect them by the power of Your Name—the Name You gave Me—so that they may be one as We are One. ¹²While I was with them, I protected them and kept them safe by that Name You gave Me. None has been lost except the one doomed to destruction so that Scripture would be fulfilled. ¹³"I am coming to You now, but I say these things while I am still in the world, so that they may have the full measure of My joy within them. ¹⁴I have given them Your word and the world has hated them, for they are not of the world any more than I am of the world. ¹⁵My prayer is not that You take them out of the world but that You protect them from the evil one. ¹⁶They are not of the world, even as I am not of it. ¹⁷Sanctify them by the truth; Your word is truth. ¹⁸As You sent Me into the world, I have sent them into the world. ¹⁹For them I sanctify myself, that they too may be truly sanctified. ²⁰"My prayer is not for them alone. I pray also for those who will believe in Me through their message, ²¹that all of them may be one, Father, just as You are in Me and I am in You. May they also be in Us so that the world may believe that You have sent Me. ²²I have given them the glory that You gave Me, that they may be one as We are One: ²³I in them and You in Me. May they be brought to complete unity to let the world know that You sent Me and have loved them even as You have loved Me."

Jesus Prayed For Oneness Among The Saints
Even though a large portion of this prayer was directed to Jesus' Disciples, we must remember that we too are Disciples

of Christ. We have been introduced to, and have embraced that message which was preserved through the ages and presented to us. Verse 20 reveals the fact that Jesus had us in mind when He presented this prayer. He offered what appears to be a theme of oneness to the Father. A familiar phrase, which denotes oneness, appears five times within this relatively short prayer. His obvious desire is for us to become one with the Father, just as He and the Father are one. Verse 21 further reveals the fact that the world will believe that Jesus is sent from the Father, when we, through the process of maturing, arrive at a state of oneness in Christ. Let us therefore submit ourselves to each other till His desire is accomplished in us. We can all rejoice in the fact that He has not left us powerless. He has given us Apostles, Prophets, Evangelists, Pastors and Teachers to bring us to that place of oneness or into the state of being 'a perfect man' Ephesians 4:9-13.

Jesus Prayed For Our Protection
Verses 14-16 – From these verses we understand that we are not of this world, but we are required to live and operate in it. We are not of this world because we live according to Him, who is not of this world. We have been placed in the world not to seek an escape from it, but to make a difference by upholding the purest principles of our faith in the midst of life. We must also remember that the spirit of this world is contrary to the spirit that works in us.

In verse 15, Jesus prayed that we would be protected from the evil one. It is inevitable that our existence in the earth will often create situations of conflict. This may sometimes result in presenting us as targets for persecution. We may often feel pressured to conform to the declining standards of the world. But Romans 12:2 reminds us that we must resist all attempts to be conformed to worldly standards, and allow the renewing of our minds to transform us, so that we may prove the acceptable and perfect will of God.

In this we can all rejoice. God is able to establish His perfect will in us in the midst of the prevailing madness in the earth. The fact remains that as believers, we will encounter many challenges living in this world. We should be comforted to know however, that our Lord has made, and continues to make intercessions on our behalf, so we may be protected from the evil one. [Verse 15] and 1 John 2:1

Apostle Paul in writing to the church at Corinth spoke about this unity, when he said:

> "That there should be no schism in the body, but that the members should have the same care for one another. And if one member suffers, all the members suffer with it; or if one member is honoured, all the members rejoice with it." [1 Corinthians 12:25-26]

Everything we think and everything we do must encompass a "We" mentality. We must continue to work out our own salvation and freely give the benefits to the corporate body. This means that all that we do in our "Christ-Centred" daily living must have a positive effect in our community and not just in ourselves.

> "Teach me Your way, O Lord, I will walk in Your truth; unite my heart to fear Your name." [Psalms 86:11]

Unity is one of our greatest strengths as a people who share one heart and one mind that are solely focused on God. David asks God to unite his heart. In essence what David is asking is for God to ensure that no other allegiances or distractions cause him to stray. It is important to realize that we can construct a corporate expression of one heart and one mind for Christ.

> "Also the hand of God was on Judah to give them singleness of heart to obey the command of the king and the leaders, at the word of the Lord." [2 Chronicles 30:12]

God is the source of unity and He can only grant it when each member is totally "sold out" to Him. This is why unity is so powerful. The Lord commands His blessing where there is unity and together as a unified people we can do more than if we were apart. The following Scriptures give us some powerful examples of what unity can accomplish.

Leviticus 26:8
> "Five of you shall chase a hundred, and a hundred of you shall put ten thousand to flight; your enemies shall fall by the sword before you."

Psalms Chapter 133
> "Behold, how good and how pleasant *it is* For brethren to dwell together in unity! ² *It is* like the precious oil upon the head, Running down on the beard, The beard of Aaron, Running down on the edge of his garments. ³ *It is* like the dew of Hermon, Descending upon the mountains of Zion; For there the LORD commanded the blessing—Life forevermore."

Principles And Promise Of Unity
The Principle is – dwelling together in unity or when He finds a family, or a marriage or a ministry or a church, and then the promise comes.

Anointing – Precious oil poured on the head down to the end

of the garment, an anointing will flow from God – This was a very special oil and was not to be used on man's flesh, however God commands it to be used wherever He finds people dwelling in unity. This oil is found in Exodus 30:22-33

Prosperity – The dew of Hermon was higher than Zion, and it was never affected by the prevailing climate of its region. Dew is always used synonymously with blessing, favour, increase, etc – Genesis 27:27-29, Deuteronomy 33:24-29, Proverbs 19:12

A Blessing of life forever more: this is not just eternal life; this is something that will have generational longevity. This is building something that will become a legacy.

The Anointing Oil – Exodus 30:22-33
"Moreover the LORD spoke to Moses, saying: "Also take for yourself quality spices--five hundred shekels of liquid myrrh, half as much sweet-smelling cinnamon [two hundred and fifty shekels], two hundred and fifty shekels of sweet-smelling cane, five hundred shekels of cassia, according to the shekel of the sanctuary, and a hin of olive oil. And you shall make from these a holy anointing oil, an ointment compounded according to the art of the perfumer. It shall be a holy anointing oil. With it you shall anoint the tabernacle of meeting and the ark of the Testimony; the table and all its utensils, the lampstand and its utensils, and the altar of incense; the altar of burnt offering with all its utensils, and the laver and its base. You shall consecrate them, that they may be most holy; whatever touches them must be holy. And you shall anoint Aaron and his sons, and consecrate them, that they may minister to Me as priests. And you shall speak to the children of Israel,

saying: 'This shall be a holy anointing oil to Me throughout your generations. It shall not be poured on man's flesh; nor shall you make any other like it, according to its composition. It is holy, and it shall be holy to you. Whoever compounds any like it, or whoever puts any of it on an outsider, shall be cut off from his people."

Ingredients Of The Anointing Oil
Myrrh: In Hebrew, the word means "Bitter" or "Free." It was taken from the gum of the dwarf tree and was supposed to flow spontaneously as the tree was cut. Pure Myrrh was bitter to the taste but had a fragrant odour. This speaks of the suffering and the resulting anointed life and ministry we experience. [Mark 15:23; John 19:39; Song of Solomon 3:6, 5:1-17; Matthew 2:11; Psalm 12:6; Esther 2:12; Zephaniah 3:8-9; Philippians 4:8; James 1:27; Revelation 22:1]. Also note that it was used as perfume [Psalm 45:8; Proverbs 7:17; Song of Solomon 3:6], in purification rites for women [Esther 2:12], as a gift for the infant Jesus [Matthew 2:11], and in embalming [signifying death to self and the flesh John 19:39].

Sweet Cinnamon: In the Hebrew it means "fragrance." This spice comes from a small evergreen [constant life] tree that has flowers with a disagreeable odour, yet the spice will improve the flavour of bitter substances [sweetness in suffering]. See Proverbs 7:17; Psalm 104:34; 119:103; Song of Solomon 2:3; Ephesians 5:2. The breath is made sweet to prophesy. [Ezekiel 37:1-14]

Sweet-smelling Cane or Calamus: In the Hebrew it means, "to stand upright, branch, reed" – [1 Kings 14:15; Ezekiel 40:3; Isaiah 42:3] – It could not grow in mire – representing the "flesh or sin life". [Isaiah 19:6]. This aromatic reed scents the air while growing. When cut down, dried, and powdered, it was used as an ingredient in the richest perfumes [the fragrance of Christ in the believer through times of crushing and shaping. Psalm 68:30]. "Branch" – the extension of the "True Vine", for the Government flows from the shoulder [Isaiah 9:6] to the Hand [Ephesians 4:11]. This is His Hand extended in the form of Apostles, Prophets, Evangelists, Pastors and Teachers.

Cassia: In the Hebrew the word means, "stoop or bow down, scrape, cleave" – worship! This plant has purple [royalty] flowers and lives at a very high [heavenly] altitude. Humility enabled by the rich anointing brings promotion [Proverbs 15:33]. This spice was also used as incense [worship] and to scent garments. Christ's regal character manifested in us as kings and priests unto God. [Revelation 1:6]. "Cleave" – Means to become one! - See Genesis 32:24-32; Ezekiel 27:19; Psalm 45:8; 2 Samuel 15:19-21; Joshua 23:4; Ruth 1:14-18.

There were some prohibitions concerning the anointing oil which were:
- Not To Be Poured On Man's Flesh. The oil was for Aaron and his sons [seed] and their spiritual ministry. [Psalm 133; 104:15; 23:5]

- Not To Be Imitated In Any Way. [The Harlot's Bed of Proverbs 7:17]

- Not To Be Put Upon A Stranger. The HOLY vessels of the Tabernacle are anointed [the Pentecostal experience is for the regenerated.]

In spite of all the restrictions of this oil, whenever the Lord sees "networking" and "unity", He responds by pouring it upon us.

> "Now the multitude of those who believed were of one heart and soul; neither did anyone say that any of the things he possessed was his own, but they had all

things in common. And with great power the apostle gave witness to the resurrection of the Lord Jesus. And great grace was upon them all." [Acts 4:32-33]

We know that since the Book of Acts was written; the Church has yet to rise up and experience the signs, wonders, and miracles that occurred in that time period. Why are we not currently in that same dimension of great grace? It is because that since that time we have not been able as a body to walk with the same degree of unity. To have one heart and one mind is to be "*in sync*" with one another, and to "*breathe spiritually*" together as one. As the local church comes together in unity and the Body of Christ unites we will see miraculous conversions [Acts 2:47], signs, wonders and miracles.

There is an awesome, powerful, militant Church rising in the earth as Apostles are being restored to take their place alongside the Prophets, Evangelists, Pastors and Teachers, to bring the Church into unity and to a place of maturity for function in the earth. It is indeed a glorious time to be alive and be connected to the purposes of the Lord. As we pray and seek the Lord we must allow God to unite our hearts so we can build accurately and that we can overtake the forces of darkness in our regions as we do the work of reconciliation.

By Walking In Present Truth:
Present Truth is the terminology that was used by the Apostle Peter to describe the revelation of Jesus Christ at that time. 2 Peter: 1:12 states

> "For this reason I will not be negligent to remind you always of these things, though you know and are established in the "*present truth*." [Italics Added]

In this particular passage of Scripture the Apostle Peter was warning the Saints of the false-teachers and erroneous doctrine that would arise, even though they were very current with what the Lord was speaking at that time. It is from this premise we coin the same phrase "Present-Truth" church. As we know, the church that was in the beginning, in the Book of Acts, had fallen away very badly during the dark ages. Most, if not all of the Five-Fold Offices as outlined in Ephesians 4:11 ["And He Himself gave some to be Apostles, some Prophets, some Evangelists, and some Pastors and some Teachers. For the equipping of the Saints for the work of the ministry, for the edifying of the Body of Christ"] had disappeared from within the structure of the visible Church. It was not until in the early 1500's when a German priest named Martin Luther, uncovered a major then "present truth", whereby "the just shall live by faith" [in that era of darkness where people were hoodwinked by the clergy into believing that potions and elixirs, and salvation of one's soul could be bought by paying the clergy]. That one present truth spawned a major reformation of the Church started, which is still in effect to this day. As time elapsed, we saw *present truth* after *present truth* being established to the Body of Christ. In the 1500's it was Justification by Faith. Before then the Church had gone through tremendous persecution and passed through the Dark Ages. It was at this point the Holy Spirit moved upon Martin Luther to stand up against the ills of his day and declare the Word of God, without compromise.

In the 1600's it was Water Baptism. Thank God for that truth being restored to the Body, as we practice it today without any contradiction.

The 1700's saw Holiness and Sanctification restored. At that time tremendous revelation was revealed concerning our Sanctification and ability to live holy lives.

With the 1880's came the restored truth on Divine Faith Healing.

We thank God for this truth, as it has found its place forever in the Church of Jesus Christ in the earth. We can walk in divine health; we can believe the Lord for healing and He has proven Himself repeatedly in this dimension, as many Saints have experienced this tremendous blessing.

At the turn of the Twentieth Century there was a tremendous truth restored to the Body of Christ, namely The Holy Spirit Baptism and Speaking with Other Tongues. This I believe was one of the most powerful moves of the Spirit of God, as we saw major "Pentecostal" denominations and several independent groups rising all over the earth proclaiming a bold new Faith that changed the then face of the Church.

Then came the 1940's when we saw the restoration of Laying On of Hands and Personal Prophecy.

In the 1950's it was Praise & Worship and Body Ministry, with Dancing. Also around that time we saw Deliverance and Evangelism breakthrough in many areas of the Body of Christ.

In the 1960's demonology was the major point of understanding that was restored to the Church, where we saw tremendous release for peoples from all walks of life.

The early 1970's brought the Discipleship, Family Life and Church Growth. In the mid to late1970's it was the Faith Message along with Prosperity and Word Teachings.

In the early 1980's we saw powerful revelation being released on the Kingdom of God and our Dominion in Christ. This revealed to us our place as kings and priest unto God and gave us the power of declaration.

Then came the restoration of Prophets to the Body of Christ

in the late 1980's and early 1990's. With this move we saw the full restoration of modern day Prophets back to the Body of Christ.

Beginning in the late 1990's we began seeing the restoration of Apostles to the Body of Christ, which is still taking place today. There is such a tremendous awareness of the government of God in the earth. It is producing in the people of God the boldness and the wisdom to stand strong in the earth today.

So then a "*Present Truth*" church is a church that is walking in the knowledge of what the Lord is speaking at the present time.

By Receiving Revelation From The Lord!
Divine revelation is absolutely vital in building accurately for the Lord and to ensure that the GATE remains open. One of the best examples of this can be found in Jesus' discourse with His early Apostles as He spoke to them for the first time concerning the Church that He was going to build!

The Scriptures reveal that on a particular day as He and His Disciples [Apostles in training] came to the region of Caesarea Philippi [Matthew 16:13], He asked them one of the most notable questions in all of His dealings with them up to that time. In the following passage of Scripture, Jesus Christ asks His disciples the pointed question, "Who do people say the Son of Man is?" And more noteworthy even is the question He posed to them, "Who do you say that I am?" – Which was correctly answered by Peter!

> "When Jesus came to the region of Caesarea Philippi, he asked his disciples, "Who do people say the Son of Man is?" 14 They replied, "Some say John the Baptist; others say Elijah; and still others, Jeremiah or one of

the prophets." 15 "But what about you?" he asked. "Who do you say I am?" 16 Simon Peter answered, "You are the Christ, the Son of the living God." 17 Jesus replied, "Blessed are you, Simon son of Jonah, for this was not revealed to you by man, but by my Father in Heaven. 18 And I tell you that you are Peter, and on this rock I will build my Church, and the gates of Hades will not overcome it. 19 I will give you the keys of the kingdom of Heaven; whatever you bind on earth will be bound in Heaven, and whatever you loose on earth will be loosed in Heaven." 20 Then he warned his disciples not to tell anyone that he was the Christ. 21 From that time on Jesus began to explain to his disciples that he must go to Jerusalem and suffer many things at the hands of the elders, chief priests and teachers of the law, and that he must be killed and on the third day be raised to life. 22 Peter took him aside and began to rebuke him. "Never, Lord!" he said. "This shall never happen to you!" 23 Jesus turned and said to Peter, "Get behind me, Satan! You are a stumbling block to me; you do not have in mind the things of God, but the things of men." 24 Then Jesus said to his disciples, "If anyone would come after me, he must deny himself and take up his cross and follow me. 25 For whoever wants to save his life will lose it, but whoever loses his life for me will find it. 26 What good will it be for a man if he gains the whole world, yet forfeits his soul? Or what can a man give in exchange for his soul?" [Matthew 16:13-26]

Jesus was trying the hearts of His disciples. He wanted to know how they felt and what they knew about Him. This to me is very powerful! Remember that this is Jesus Christ, the Man who knew what was in the hearts of all men. He was the Man Sent from God, and yet He prodded His disciples to answer a seemingly redundant question in wanting to know what His disciples thought about Him!

This was indeed a loaded question and Jesus Christ as The Apostle had to be sure that they themselves were convinced beyond the shadow of a doubt as to Who He was. He certainly knew Who He was. Jesus Christ had the God confidence of knowing who He was and He knew His purpose as well as His Source. The Apostles' response to that question began to reveal a sad lack of revelation knowledge of Who He really was. "Some say John the Baptist; others say Elijah; and still others, Jeremiah or one of the prophets;" were some of their answers. Then out of the mouth of Peter came the following: "You are the Christ, the Son of The Living God"; and with great elation Jesus Christ declared that the source of Peter's revelation was not from flesh and blood but that he had indeed heard from His Father who was in Heaven.

Jesus declared to him, "flesh and blood did not reveal this to you." The Greek word for "reveal" in this case is translated as the word apokalupto. Our word Apocalypse stems from this same word and it signifies to uncover, unveil of all things. Only one person out of the twelve was hearing from God that day and it was Peter!

Peter's name in the Greek meant little rock and Jesus Christ said to him, "you are known as "little rock", however, upon the Big Rock of this revelation that you just received I will be building My Church and the gates of hell will not be able to prevail against It!"

This was the very first time in the New Testament or during the time of Jesus Christ's walk on the earth that He referred to His building of The Church. Up to that time all He spoke about was The Kingdom of God and now He introduces this brand new concept of The Church.

When Christ proclaimed that Peter would build the Church, it only stood to reason that on the Day of Pentecost, Apostle Peter was the first one to speak to the Church and was able to correctly discern what was occurring; when he said after the Holy Spirit had come upon them: Acts 2:14-16

> "But Peter, standing up with the eleven, raised his voice and said to them, "Men of Judea and all who dwell in Jerusalem, let this be known to you, and heed my words. 15 For these are not drunk, as you suppose, since it is only the third hour of the day. 16 But this is what was spoken by the prophet Joel:"

By Moving Accurately Into God's Purposes!
Let me briefly say this as it regards to God's Purpose; it is exactly that *"God's Purpose"* and not our own purpose. It isn't made to order, it is ordained from the beginning of time. Purpose is God's counsel, advice, planning, consultation, and deliberation. With purpose, we consider what His purpose is and not what our interpretation is of His Purpose.

So to move accurately in His Purpose we must first go back to what HE had originally purposed, patterned, and positioned us for. For our purpose really begins with HIS Purpose: and that means for what we have been purposely ordained for in the earth.

Also remember this: Our Purpose is centered in Jesus Christ according to Ephesians 1:18

> "...the eyes of your understanding being enlightened; that you may know what is the hope of His calling, what

are the riches of the glory of His inheritance in the saints..."

By Allowing The Lord To Come Strongly Into Our Midst And Manifest Himself! For it is only where the Spirit of the Lord is, that there is true liberty!

1 Corinthians 3:8-18
> "But if the ministry of death, written *and* engraved on stones, was glorious, so that the children of Israel could not look steadily at the face of Moses because of the glory of his countenance, which *glory* was passing away, 8 how will the ministry of the Spirit not be more glorious? 9 For if the ministry of condemnation *had* glory, the ministry of righteousness exceeds much more in glory. 10 For even what was made glorious had no glory in this respect, because of the glory that excels. 11 For if what is passing away *was* glorious, what remains *is* much more glorious. 12 Therefore, since we have such hope, we use great boldness of speech— 13 unlike Moses, *who* put a veil over his face so that the children of Israel could not look steadily at the end of what was passing away. 14 But their minds were blinded. For until this day the same veil remains unlifted in the reading of the Old Testament, because the *veil* is taken away in Christ. 15 But even to this day, when Moses is read, a veil lies on their heart. 16 Nevertheless when one turns to the Lord, the veil is taken away. 17 *Now the Lord is the Spirit; and where the Spirit of the Lord is, there is liberty.* 18 But we all, with unveiled face, beholding as in a mirror the glory of the Lord, are being transformed into the same image from glory to glory, just as by the Spirit of the Lord." [Italics Added]

It is the Presence of the Lord that gives us great joy, and as we know "the joy of the Lord is our strength..."

"You will show me the path of life; In Your presence

is fullness of joy; At Your right hand *are* pleasures forevermore." [Psalms 16:11]

> "Then he said to them, "Go your way, eat the fat, drink the sweet, and send portions to those for whom nothing is prepared; for *this* day *is* holy to our Lord. Do not sorrow, for the joy of the LORD is your strength." [Nehemiah 8:10]

By Constantly Changing Into The Image And Likeness Of Jesus! This is the sole purpose of the Believer and the Church, and that is to become more like Jesus. The more we become like Him, the better we are able to represent Him in the earth. It is in beholding HIM that we are then changed:

> "But we all, with unveiled face, beholding as in a mirror the glory of the Lord, are being transformed into the same image from glory to glory, just as by the Spirit of the Lord." [1 Corinthians 3:18]

Very Strong Focus – Causing The Families Of The Earth To Be Blessed:

> "Also your descendants shall be as the dust of the earth; you shall spread abroad to the west and the east, to the north and the south; and in you and in your seed all the families of the earth shall be blessed." [Genesis 28:14]

In order to fulfill the God given mandate of any local church there must be *FOCUS*.

Let Us Briefly Explore The Meaning Of The Word "Focus": *Focus* – a concentration of intent upon specific mandates or purposes. It is similar to a *magnifying glass being used to set paper on fire using the sun's rays.*

Focus is one of the valuable keys if one is to succeed and this applies to each and every area of one's life.

A Loss of Focus causes one's strength to depart and defeat to step in. This is one of the enemy main tactics – that of causing us to loose Focus[1].

In the Scripture passages below, we read about two case studies, one resulting from what the power Focus brings, and the other resulting from a loss or absence of Focus:

2 Kings Chapter 9: The Power of Focus. [Jehu]
Jehu's Anointing:
> "And Elisha the Prophet called one of the sons of the Prophets, and said to him, "Get yourself ready, take this flask of oil in your hand, and go to Ramoth Gilead. Now when you arrive at that place, look there for Jehu the son of Jehoshaphat, the son of Nimshi, and go in and make him rise up from among his associates, and take him to an *inner room*. Then take the flask of oil, and pour it on his head, and say, 'Thus says the LORD: "I have anointed you king over Israel."' Then open the door and flee, and do not delay." So the young man, the servant of the Prophet, went to Ramoth Gilead. And when he arrived, there were the captains of the army sitting; and he said, "I have a message for you, Commander." Jehu said, "For which one of us?" And he said, "For you, Commander." Then he arose and went into the house. And he poured the oil on his head, and said to him, "Thus says the LORD God of Israel: 'I have anointed you king over the people of the LORD, over Israel. *You shall strike down the house of Ahab your master*, that I may avenge the blood of My servants the Prophets, and the blood of all the servants

---

[1] Hebrews 10:35-39

of the LORD, at the hand of Jezebel. For the whole house of Ahab shall perish; and I will cut off from Ahab all the males in Israel, the house of Baasha the son of Ahijah. *The dogs shall eat Jezebel* on the plot of ground at Jezreel, and there shall be none to bury her.' "And he opened the door and fled." [2 Kings 9:1-10 Italics Added]

Points Of Note
- Elisha himself does not anoint Jehu – he sends one of the sons of the Prophets – verse 1! This speaks about the power of relationship within the framework of training, accountability, submission, etc. There are some things we will never be able to do for God apart from possessing these qualities!

- Jehu was separated from his fellowmen and taken into an "[2]Inner Room" – verse 2! This "Inner Room Anointing" is very vital in the call of God. This is where we receive the power to do works of service. It is here we receive our mandate, revelation and the technology for success. Remember what Jesus instructed us in Matthew 10:27 "Whatever I tell you in the dark, speak in the light; and what you hear in the ear, preach on the housetops.

- Jehu then receives his general mandate in 2 Kings 9:6 "I have anointed you king over the people of the Lord, over Israel" – this is very general! It is similar to being anointed and being told "for I anointed you to be a man/woman of God, and I have released to

---

[2] For more on this "internal work" you can read the author's new book "Internal Reformation – Mark Of A True Disciple", which is with the Publishers, Word Alive Press. Ordering details at the end of this book!

you gifts and abilities to accomplish all that I have for you to do, etc, etc."

- Jehu then receives his specific mandate: 2 Kings 9:6 "You shall strike down the house of Ahab your master, that I may avenge the blood of My servants the Prophets, and the blood of all the servants of the LORD, at the hand of Jezebel." This specific mandate has its root in a previous sequence of events, [which most times is the case, as God always has a plan and purpose in mind]. God did this because of the following:

"And it came to pass after these things that Naboth the Jezreelite had a vineyard which was in Jezreel, next to the palace of Ahab king of Samaria. So Ahab spoke to Naboth, saying, "Give me your vineyard, that I may have it for a vegetable garden, because it is near, next to my house; and for it I will give you a vineyard better than it. Or, if it seems good to you, I will give you its worth in money." But Naboth said to Ahab, "The LORD forbid that I should give the inheritance of my fathers to you!" So Ahab went into his house sullen and displeased because of the word which Naboth the Jezreelite had spoken to him; for he had said, "I will not give you the inheritance of my fathers." And he lay down on his bed, and turned away his face, and would eat no food. But Jezebel his wife came to him, and said to him, "Why is your spirit so sullen that you eat no food?" He said to her, "Because I spoke to Naboth the Jezreelite, and said to him, 'Give me your vineyard for money; or else, if it pleases you, I will give you another vineyard for it.' And he answered, 'I will not give you my vineyard.'

"Then Jezebel his wife said to him, "You now exercise authority over Israel! Arise, eat food, and let your heart be cheerful; I will give you the vineyard of Naboth the Jezreelite." And she wrote letters in Ahab's name, sealed them with his seal, and sent the letters to the elders and the nobles who were dwelling in the city with Naboth. She wrote in the letters, saying, Proclaim a fast, and seat Naboth with high honour among the people; and seat two men, scoundrels, before him to bear witness against him, saying, "You have blasphemed God and the king." Then take him out, and stone him, that he may die. So the men of his city, the elders and nobles who were inhabitants of his city, did as Jezebel had sent to them, as it was written in the letters, which she had sent to them. They proclaimed a fast, and seated Naboth with high as it was written in the letters, which she had sent to them. They proclaimed a fast, and seated Naboth with high honour among the people. And two men, scoundrels, came in and sat before him; and the scoundrels witnessed against him, against Naboth, in the presence of the people, saying, "Naboth has blasphemed God and the king!" Then they took him outside the city and stoned him with stones, so that he died. Then they sent to Jezebel, saying, "Naboth has been stoned and is dead." And it came to pass, when Jezebel heard that Naboth had been stoned and was dead, that Jezebel said to Ahab, "Arise, take possession of the vineyard of Naboth the Jezreelite, which he refused to give you for money; for Naboth is not alive, but dead." So it was, when Ahab heard that Naboth was dead, that Ahab got up and went down to take possession of the vineyard of Naboth the Jezreelite. Then the word of the LORD came to Elijah the Tishbite, saying, "Arise, go down to meet Ahab king of Israel, who lives in Samaria. There he is, in the vineyard of Naboth, where he has gone down to take possession of it. You shall speak to him, saying, 'Thus says the LORD: "Have you murdered and also taken possession?" 'And you shall speak to him, saying, 'Thus says the LORD: "In the place where dogs licked the blood of Naboth, dogs shall lick your blood, even yours." '"Then Ahab said to Elijah, "Have you found me, O my enemy?" And he answered, "I have found you, because you have sold yourself to do evil in the sight of the LORD: 'Behold, I will bring calamity on you. I will take away your posterity, and will cut off from Ahab every male in Israel, both bond and free. I will make your house like the house of Jeroboam the son of Nebat, and like the house of Baasha the son of Ahijah, because of the provocation with which you have provoked Me to anger, and made Israel sin.' "And concerning Jezebel the LORD also spoke, saying, 'The dogs shall eat Jezebel by the wall of Jezreel.' "The dogs shall eat whoever belongs to Ahab and dies in the city, and the birds of the air shall eat whoever dies in the field." [1 Kings 21:1-24]

We would do well to take a closer look at how Jehu accomplished the God given mandate that was placed upon him. We want to approach this from the understanding that the [3]godly kings in the Old Testament were a type of the

---

[3] You can read the author's books on the apostolic, more information and ordering details at the end of this book.

Apostles in the New Testament and this correlation can give us valuable operational technology for Apostles today.

Remember that during Jehu's reign, Israel was unfortunately being governed by the impure and incapable leadership in the Jezebel/Ahab's administration. The Word of God declares:

> "*Woe to you, O land, when your king is a child*, And your princes feast in the morning! Blessed are you, O land, when your king is the son of nobles, And your princes feast at the proper time--For strength and not for drunkenness!" [Ecclesiastes 10:16-17 Italics Added]

Jezebel [representing *a false governmental voice*] was in power and thereby released all kinds of demonic powers over the land. demonic powers were in the gates of the city and the Lord had established a covenant with Abraham that the people of God would always possess the gates of their enemies.

> "Then the Angel of the LORD called to Abraham a second time out of heaven, and said: "By Myself I have sworn, says the LORD, because you have done this thing, and have not withheld your son, your only son--blessing I will bless you, and in multiplying I will multiply your descendants as the stars of the heaven and as the sand which is on the seashore; *and your descendants shall possess the gate of their enemies.*" [Genesis 22:15-17 Italics Added]

> "And they blessed Rebekah and said to her: "Our sister, may you become The mother of thousands of ten thousands; And may *your descendants possess the gates of those who hate them.*" [Genesis 24:60 Italics Added]

In establishing Jehu as king [*a type of the apostolic*] the Lord would ensure that the enemy was defeated and true governance returned to Israel.

In like manner we are being raised up by God to take away the authority from demonic elders and establish the government of God in the earth! Jehu was anointed in the *"inner room"* where he was equipped for service! He then steps out and fulfils Elijah's mandate to the letter. In order to accomplish this he had to make sure that he was intensely focused! He was about to confront one of the strongest demonic powers of the day. It is no different today! In order to fulfil any God given mandate, one must be intensely *focused*.

As we read through the account of Jehu's fulfilment of the prophetic word given to him, we will realize how focused he was in accomplishing the task at hand[4]. Conversely a study of the life of Saul accurately reflects the results of the [5]loss of focus in fulfilling a God-given mandate.

1 Samuel Chapter 15: The Results of a Loss of Focus. [King Saul.] The Scripture speaks for itself with regards to the result of King Saul's loss of focus. He was commanded to destroy Amalek from under Heaven, but lost his focus and spared Agag, king of the Amalekites [which by interpretation means "flesh!"]

Saul Spares King Agag:
> "Samuel also said to Saul, "The LORD sent me to anoint you king over His people, over Israel. Now therefore, heed the voice of the words of the LORD. 2 Thus says the LORD of hosts: 'I will punish Amalek

---

[4] 2 Kings Chapter 9
[5] 1 Samuel Chapter 15

for what he did to Israel, how he ambushed him on the way when he came up from Egypt. ³ Now go and attack Amalek, and utterly destroy all that they have, and do not spare them. But kill both man and woman, infant and nursing child, ox and sheep, camel and donkey.'" ⁴ So Saul gathered the people together and numbered them in Telaim, two hundred thousand foot soldiers and ten thousand men of Judah. ⁵ And Saul came to a city of Amalek, and lay in wait in the valley. ⁶ Then Saul said to the Kenites, "Go, depart, get down from among the Amalekites, lest I destroy you with them. For you showed kindness to all the children of Israel when they came up out of Egypt." So the Kenites departed from among the Amalekites. ⁷ And Saul attacked the Amalekites, from Havilah all the way to Shur, which is east of Egypt. ⁸ He also took Agag king of the Amalekites alive, and utterly destroyed all the people with the edge of the sword. ⁹ But Saul and the people spared Agag and the best of the sheep, the oxen, the fatlings, the lambs, and all *that was* good, and were unwilling to utterly destroy them. But everything despised and worthless, that they utterly destroyed."

Saul Rejected As King:
"¹⁰ Now the word of the LORD came to Samuel, saying, ¹¹ "I greatly regret that I have set up Saul *as* king, for he has turned back from following Me, and has not performed My commandments." And it grieved Samuel, and he cried out to the LORD all night. ¹² So when Samuel rose early in the morning to meet Saul, it was told Samuel, saying, "Saul went to Carmel, and indeed, he set up a monument for himself; and he has gone on around, passed by, and gone down to Gilgal." ¹³ Then Samuel went to Saul,

and Saul said to him, "Blessed *are* you of the LORD! I have performed the commandment of the LORD." 14 But Samuel said, "What then *is* this bleating of the sheep in my ears, and the lowing of the oxen which I hear?" 15 And Saul said, "They have brought them from the Amalekites; for the people spared the best of the sheep and the oxen, to sacrifice to the LORD your God; and the rest we have utterly destroyed." 16 Then Samuel said to Saul, "Be quiet! And I will tell you what the LORD said to me last night." And he said to him, "Speak on." 17 So Samuel said, "When you *were* little in your own eyes, *were* you not head of the tribes of Israel? And did not the LORD anoint you king over Israel? 18 Now the LORD sent you on a mission, and said, 'Go, and utterly destroy the sinners, the Amalekites, and fight against them until they are consumed.' 19 Why then did you not obey the voice of the LORD? Why did you swoop down on the spoil, and do evil in the sight of the LORD?" 20 And Saul said to Samuel, "But I have obeyed the voice of the LORD, and gone on the mission on which the LORD sent me, and brought back Agag king of Amalek; I have utterly destroyed the Amalekites. 21 But the people took of the plunder, sheep and oxen, the best of the things which should have been utterly destroyed, to sacrifice to the LORD your God in Gilgal." 22 So Samuel said: "Has the LORD *as great* delight in burnt offerings and sacrifices, As in obeying the voice of the LORD? Behold, to obey is better than sacrifice, *And* to heed than the fat of rams. 23 For rebellion *is as* the sin of witchcraft, And stubbornness *is as* iniquity and idolatry. Because you have rejected the word of the LORD, He also has rejected you from *being* king." 24 Then Saul said to Samuel, "I have sinned, for I have transgressed the commandment of the LORD and your words, because I feared the people and obeyed their voice. ²⁵ Now therefore, please pardon my sin, and return with me, that I may worship the LORD." ²⁶ But Samuel said to Saul, "I will not return with you, for you have rejected the word of the LORD, and the LORD has rejected you from being king over Israel." ²⁷ And as Samuel turned around to go away, *Saul* seized the edge of his robe, and it tore. ²⁸ So Samuel said to him, "The LORD has torn the kingdom of Israel from you today, and has given it to a neighbor of yours, *who is* better than you. ²⁹ And also the Strength of Israel will not lie nor relent. For He *is* not a man, that He should relent." ³⁰ Then he said, "I have sinned; *yet* honor me now, please, before the elders of my people and before Israel, and return with me, that I may worship the LORD your God." ³¹ So Samuel turned back after Saul, and Saul worshiped the LORD. ³² Then Samuel said, "Bring Agag king of the Amalekites here to me." So Agag came to him cautiously. And Agag said, "Surely the bitterness of death is past." ³³ But Samuel said, "As your sword has made women childless, so shall your mother be childless among women." And Samuel hacked Agag in pieces before the LORD in Gilgal. ³⁴ Then Samuel went to Ramah, and Saul went up to his house at Gibeah of Saul. ³⁵ And Samuel went no more to see Saul until the day of his death. Nevertheless Samuel mourned for Saul, and the LORD regretted that He had made Saul king over Israel."

The Fortress Church Has Many Resources Or Resource Personnel – As The Dust Of The Earth, Spreading To Every Direction – Verses 13-14!

"And behold, the LORD stood above it and said: "I *am* the LORD God of Abraham your father and the God of Isaac; the land on which you lie I will give to you and your descendants. 14 Also your descendants shall be as the dust of the earth; you shall spread abroad to the west and the east, to the north and the south; and in you and in your seed all the families of the earth shall be blessed."

It Is A Visible Church – Angels Are Ascending And Descending From It – Verse 12

"Then he dreamed, and behold, a ladder *was* set up on the earth, and its top reached to heaven; and there the angels of God were ascending and descending on it." – Notice the order!

Take careful notice of the order of this angelic activity; it begins from the church and goes to Heaven; they are ascending and descending...

Has A Strong Impact Upon The Spirit Realm – Verse 12

"Then he dreamed, and behold, a ladder *was* set up on the earth, and its top reached to heaven; and there the angels of God were ascending and descending on it."

Interestingly the same promise was given to Abraham: Genesis 22:8-18!

"And Abraham said, "My son, God will provide for Himself the lamb for a burnt offering." So the two of them went together. 9 Then they came to the place of which God had told him. And Abraham built an altar there and placed the wood in order; and he bound Isaac his son and laid him on the altar, upon the wood. 10 And Abraham stretched out his hand and took the knife to slay his son. 11 But the Angel of the LORD called to him from heaven and said, "Abraham,

Abraham!" So he said, "Here I am." ¹² And He said, "Do not lay your hand on the lad, or do anything to him; for now I know that you fear God, since you have not withheld your son, your only *son*, from Me." ¹³ Then Abraham lifted his eyes and looked, and there behind *him was* a ram caught in a thicket by its horns. So Abraham went and took the ram, and offered it up for a burnt offering instead of his son. ¹⁴ And Abraham called the name of the place, The-LORD-Will-Provide; as it is said *to* this day, "In the Mount of the LORD it shall be provided." ¹⁵ Then the Angel of the LORD called to Abraham a second time out of heaven, ¹⁶ and said: "By Myself I have sworn, says the LORD, because you have done this thing, and have not withheld your son, your only *son*— ¹⁷ blessing I will bless you, and multiplying I will multiply your descendants as the stars of the heaven and as the sand which *is* on the seashore; and your descendants shall possess the gate of their enemies. ¹⁸ In your seed all the nations of the earth shall be blessed, because you have obeyed My voice."

Just a brief note here: I believe that this incident was a type of the guarantee of the finished work of Calvary. Here Abraham, a type of the Heavenly Father was asked to give up his son Isaac as a type of the *"Perfect Lamb"*! However, he was spared from doing it as Jesus Christ the Son of the Living God would come hundred of years later at the appointed time and would actually go to the Cross and be crucified as the *"Perfect Lamb of God"*!

The Fortress Church Will Eventually Impact The Politics, Economics And Lifestyle Of A Nation – Verse 14!

"Also your descendants shall be as the dust of the earth; you shall spread abroad to the west and the east, to the north and the south; and in you and in your seed all the families of the earth shall be blessed."

It Has What We Call A Governmental Anointing – Verse 14
"Also your descendants shall be as the dust of the earth; you shall spread abroad to the west and the east, to the north and the south; and in you and in your seed all the families of the earth shall be blessed."

Remember this, that The Church is the True Government of God, as recorded in Isaiah 9:6-7!

"For unto us a Child is born, Unto us a Son is given; And the government will be upon His shoulder. And His name will be called Wonderful, Counsellor, Mighty God, Everlasting Father, Prince of Peace. 7 Of the increase of *His* government and peace *There will be* no end, Upon the throne of David and over His kingdom, To order it and establish it with judgment and justice From that time forward, even forever. The zeal of the Lord of hosts will perform this."

☞ **CHAPTER 2**

DYNAMICS OF THE FORTRESS CHURCH II

Throughout the Bible, the *Fortress Church* is epitomized as a structure that stands, builds and gives mankind the true picture of just what a fortress church is as presented and woven amidst the words therein. We begin with the Psalms...

The Psalmist View
Psalms Chapter 48 NIV

"Great is the LORD, and most worthy of praise, *in the city of our God*, his holy mountain [the Church]. *It is beautiful in its loftiness, the joy of the whole earth.* Like the utmost heights of Zaphon is Mount Zion, the city of the Great King [the Church]. God is in her citadels; he has shown himself to be her [the Church] *fortress*. When *the kings joined forces, when they advanced together, they saw [her – the Church] and were astounded; they fled in terror.* Trembling seized them there, pain like that of a woman in labour. You destroyed them like ships of Tarshish shattered by an east wind. As we have heard, so have we seen in the city of the LORD Almighty, in the city of our God: God makes her secure forever [the Church]. Selah Within *your temple,* [*the Church*] O God, we meditate on your unfailing love. Like your name, O God, your praise reaches to the ends of the earth; your right hand is filled with righteousness. Mount Zion rejoices, the villages of Judah are glad because of your judgements.

In describing what I believe is the Church of Jesus Christ, the Psalmist declared that: God is Great in the *Fortress Church* and worthy of all praise. It is beautiful in its *loftiness or elevation*.

Loftiness – Not to be confused with the common definition of "loftiness", loftiness here is used in the sense of position, i.e. a place of elevation, not one of being proud or haughty. It is build upon Mount Zion on the sides of the North a true place of elevation.

Mt Zion, also know as The Church is beautiful because of Its elevation, Its loftiness, Its position! As a matter of fact, the terminology "Mt Zion on the sides of the North" in Hebrew depicts Elevation or Height.

Elevation or Height is very important in the spirit realm. As seen in Isaiah 2:1-4, the world is going up to Zion, [The "*Fortress Church*"]! Obviously from this Scripture, this "up" lifestyle is not that which is consistent with the world; but rather it must be different and should cause the world to turn their heads and take notice at this Church. Of note, this passage refers to "in every generation" and certainly we qualify to be this type of church.

It is imperative that we understand that the spirit realm runs by rank or position. The Apostle Paul in writing to the church at Ephesus made this very clear:

> "Therefore I also, after I heard of your faith in the Lord Jesus and your love for all the saints, do not cease to give thanks for you, making mention of you in my prayers: that the God of our Lord Jesus Christ, the Father of glory, may give to you the spirit of wisdom and revelation in the knowledge of Him, the eyes of your understanding being enlightened; that you may know what is the hope of His calling, what

are the riches of the glory of His inheritance in the saints, and *what is the exceeding greatness of His power toward us who believe*, according to the working of His mighty power which He worked in Christ when He raised Him from the dead and seated Him at His right hand in the heavenly places, *far above all principality and power and might and dominion, and every name that is named, not only in this age but also in that which is to come. And He put all things under His feet, and gave Him to be head over all things to the church, which is His body, the fullness of Him who fills all in all.* And you He made alive, who were dead in trespasses and sins, in which you once walked according to the course of this world, according to the prince of the power of the air, the spirit who now works in the sons of disobedience, among whom also we all once conducted ourselves in the lusts of our flesh, fulfilling the desires of the flesh and of the mind, and were by nature children of wrath, just as the others. But God, who is rich in mercy, because of His great love with which He loved us, even when we were dead in trespasses, *made us alive together with Christ* [by grace you have been saved], and raised us up together, and made us sit together in the heavenly places in Christ Jesus." [Ephesians 1:15-2:6 Italics Added]

In describing the Lord's position, the Apostle Paul uses very strong and expressive language – far above all! Jesus is not just above all principalities, powers, might and dominion; He is at an extreme distance above them. Apostles are mandated to bring the Church into a clear understanding of this fact. They want to see every Believer conformed to the Image of Christ. The Apostle Paul's earnest cry for the Saints was that they saw, comprehended and entered into the awesome revelation of "Christ in you the hope of glory." Paul accentuated that fact when he went on to establish that when Jesus was positioned far above all, we were raised up together with Him! We are positioned in the same place that Jesus is and we must know and realize this.

Let me reemphasize the fact that the spirit realm works by an internal sense of your position. Position is key. We just have to know this and be very conscious of the fact, because the devil will try everything possible to negate this fact.

Jesus is lifted up over every other name. He has the highest rank or position. When we pray in the Name of Jesus it is from a position we are praying, and not just a religious phrase we are using – not just something we add on to our prayers for power.

We pray in Jesus Name! – It Is A Spiritual Location From Which We Function – It Is A Lifestyle – It Is An Identity!

We cannot function in the spirit realm with condemnation – we must be confident in our position in Him – we must know our significance in Him! This is the mentality of apostolic people in the *"Fortress Church."*

The Reality Of What Jesus Accomplished
"Therefore He says: "When He ascended on high, He led captivity captive, And gave gifts to men." [Now this, "He ascended"--what does it mean but that He also first descended into the lower parts of the earth? He who descended is also the One who ascended far above all the heavens, that He might fill all things.] [Ephesians 4:8-10]

- He descended then He arose!

- He went into the deepest depths of hell and then arose!
- Every place where the soles of your feet will tread it is yours!
- Jesus has control and authority over every realm from heaven to the lowest part of hell!
- We as Born-Again Believers have the same authority because of Jesus – We sit with Him in Heavenly places!

For those of you reading this book who still have problems with condemnation, hear me – this is the hour for you to break away from your past life of condemnation! Remember He ascended that He might fill all things! And He has taken us with Him!

The next facet we see of this *"Fortress Church"* is the intensity of Her warfare, as the demonic kings of the earth join forces to seek Her destruction:

> "When the kings joined forces, when they advanced together, they saw [her] and were astounded; they fled in terror. Trembling seized them there, pain like that of a woman in labour. You destroyed them like ships of Tarshish shattered by an east wind." [Psalm 48:4-7]

These kings of the earth are demonic. They assemble and advance against the *"Fortress Church"*. We are not talking little insignificant devils that cause Pastors to divorce their wives and marry their secretaries. No! These are big devils; they are high-ranking demonic powers and they will seek to dismantle, disjoint, and completely destroy the *"Fortress Church"*. This is why every local church needs to have the apostolic dimension in it. Part of the apostolic career is the ability to dismantle demonic thrones and powers. The apostolic anointing can penetrate and dismantle inaccurate mindsets and thought patterns established by these "demonic kings of the earth". The Apostle Paul effectively describes this apostolic dimension when he said:

> "For the weapons of our warfare are not carnal but mighty in God for pulling down strongholds, casting down arguments and every high thing that exalts itself against the knowledge of God, bringing every thought into captivity to the obedience of Christ, and being ready to punish all disobedience when your obedience is fulfilled. [2 Corinthians 10:4-6]

This Apostolic Church [*Fortress Church*] that is rising in the earth, is awesome. The demonic kings of the earth saw it [the implication here is that they saw and understood what was happening. They saw and heard.] They scrutinized it; they carefully checked out this *"Fortress Church"*; this stronghold – this was not a casual looking; this was intense. Hake a look at Ephesians 3:8-12

> "...this grace was given, that I should preach among the Gentiles the unsearchable riches of Christ, and *to make all see what is the fellowship of the mystery*, which from the beginning of the ages has been hidden in God who created all things through Jesus Christ; *to the intent that now the manifold wisdom of God might be made known by the church to the principalities and powers in the heavenly places, according to the eternal purpose which He accomplished in Christ Jesus our Lord*, in whom we have boldness and access with confidence through faith in Him." [Italics Added]

Some may argue that the reference to principalities and powers is not demonic but righteous angels. This cannot be, as every other [6]mention of that term denotes demonic activity.

When these demonic kings saw and heard, they marvelled! They were astonished. They were in confusion and consternation.

The kingdom of darkness is tormented by a *"Fortress Church"* – the result, was that they fled in terror [NIV], this is what a *"Fortress Church"* does to the enemy. The Church of the Lord Jesus Christ is rising in the earth, to Her place of pre-ordained strength and beauty. There are more dimensions to this Church that is emerging.

> "As we have heard, So we have seen In the city of the LORD of hosts, In the city of our God: God will establish it forever. Selah" [Psalm 48:8]

As We Have Heard So Have We Seen
In some churches, there has been too much hearing and no seeing, and the Lord God Almighty is changing all of that. This new "apostolic reformation" as some would prefer to call it, is changing the face of the Church. In this *Fortress Church* the face of man is disappearing and instead is becoming the place where you can SEE the Lord. This type of Church is not built around programs or men or personalities; it is built on vision that is centred in the Lord.

It Is A Place Where The Walk Matches The Talk! It is an Apostolic Church that can decode and bring to reality the mysteries of the Lord. Similar to the Apostle Peter on the Day of Pentecost in Acts 2:14-16:

> "But Peter, standing up with the eleven, lifted up his voice, and said unto them, Ye men of Judaea, and all

---

[6] Romans 8:38, Ephesians 6:12, Colossians 1:16 & Colossians 2:15

ye that dwell at Jerusalem, be this known unto you, and hearken to my words: *For these are not drunken, as ye suppose, seeing it is but the third hour of the day. But this is that which was spoken by the prophet Joel.*"
[KJV Italics Added]

"What you have heard, we now bring into manifestation," Apostle Peter declared, and we need to do the same. The *"Fortress Church"* allows the Word to become flesh and live through the Saints. This is why we must allow the Apostles to return and do what the Lord has assigned to them so that this Church, this *"Fortress Church"* can fully rise in the earth.

This *Fortress Church* progresses into a place of what can be best described as Mature Joy, a joy that reaches beyond the initial [7]Joy of Salvation.

Mature Joy
"Within your temple, O God, we meditate on your unfailing love. Like your name, O God, your praise reaches to the ends of the earth; your right hand is filled with righteousness. *Mount Zion rejoices, the villages of Judah are glad because of your judgments.*
[Psalm 48:9-11 Italics Added]

This type of joy is produced as a result of God's judgement. Judgement here is not speaking about God's punishment. It is referring to the Lord's justice or decision. This is the joy that results from an obedient lifestyle – that comes from righteous living. This is what happens as the Apostles come alongside the other "Five-Fold" ministry gifts, assisting in the perfecting of the Saints, bringing us into the fullness of the measure of the stature of Jesus Christ.

---

[7] Isaiah 12:3

Remember it is Righteousness, Peace and Joy in the Holy Ghost! We must all be in the grip of a mighty process, a process of change through the Hands of a Mighty God!

Again, there is Joy because of God's Judgement! Not God's punishment, but rather it is referring to the Lord's Justice or Decision. God becoming the Sovereign Lord over our lives!

John 9:39-41 best explains this to us:
> "Jesus said, "For judgment I have come into this world, so that the blind will see and those who see will become blind." 40 Some Pharisees who were with him heard him say this and asked, "What? Are we blind too?"

Jesus began to preach and the very first thing He says is "For judgement I am come into the world..."

Judgement:
- It is the Greek word krino – "to decide," "give a verdict," "declare an opinion!"
- Another Greek word – anakrino "to investigate," "scrutinize!"
- Also the word diakrino – "to discriminate," "distinguish!"

It is also where we get our English word criterion:
- Criterion – decisive factor; a standard for measurement, etc!

Most times when we hear this word Judgement the first thing we think about is a negative principle of judging falsely. However, when you hear this word I want you think of JUSTICE!

Jesus was bringing true Justice – He was saying: The real justice here is that I came in the flesh to be the criterion – the standard by which all things are judged – the way – the truth – the light – I am

He whom all else shall be measured by [in essence He was telling the Pharisees, it was His Judgement and not Moses'].

Now you have to understand, a Judge is one who mediates between two parties in order to arrive at a fair conclusion – He is a go between. For example there are times here in British Columbia, Canada where I live, when we have a Public Service strike because Union and Management cannot come to a fair settlement and so the government steps in and appoints a mediator [Someone like Mr. Vince Ready] to be a broker or a go between or an umpire or arbitrator [between labour and management] in order to arrive at a fair settlement. The same with JESUS – there was an impasse between GOD and Man and Jesus was brought to act as a mediator to bring judgement or justice in the matter – this is why the Word says:

1 Timothy 2:5
"For there is one God and one mediator between God and mankind, the man Christ Jesus…"

Hebrews 3:1-5
"Therefore, holy brothers and sisters, who share in the heavenly calling, fix your thoughts on Jesus, whom we acknowledge as our apostle and high priest. ² He was faithful to the one who appointed him, just as Moses was faithful in all God's house. ³ Jesus has been found worthy of greater honour than Moses, just as the builder of a house has greater honour than the house itself. ⁴ For every house is built by someone, but God is the builder of everything. ⁵ "Moses was faithful as a servant in all God's house," bearing witness to what would be spoken by God in the future."

Jesus is the Mediator; He is the STANDARD; Not Moses; not

Abraham; not Solomon; not anyone else JESUS, ALONE IS THE TRUE STANDARD!!!

So in essence Jesus declared – this is my Judgement in this matter – You who declare that you can see [in essence thinks he can see] is blind… And those who cannot see I will cause to see.

This Mature Joy is produced when we walk accurate in God. When we allow our steps to be ordered and ordained by Him. It is maturity when we can submit to the Hand and Process of Almighty God – it is immaturity when we cannot submit and be brought under the Mighty Hand of God, and under the scrutiny of God.

This Maturity Produces Generational Blessings!
The *"Fortress Church"* is an exemplar model or prototype Church. We must declare that it is possible to build a Strong Church. A Church that reclaims its Generational Power, a Church that can last through the generations, with a sense of purpose and direction.

The *"Fortress Church"* seeks to destroy the spirit that causes the next generation to be lost. That happened under Joshua and so many others, throughout Church history.

Judges 2:8-12
> "Now Joshua the son of Nun, the servant of the LORD, died when he was one hundred and ten years old. And they buried him within the border of his inheritance at Timnath Heres, in the mountains of Ephraim, on the north side of Mount Gaash. When all that generation had been gathered to their fathers, another generation arose after them who did not know the LORD nor the work, which He had done for

Israel. Then the children of Israel did evil in the sight of the LORD, and served the Baals; and they forsook the LORD God of their fathers, who had brought them out of the land of Egypt; and they followed other gods from among the gods of the people who were all around them, and they bowed down to them; and they provoked the LORD to anger." [Italics Added]

From that time the Lord allowed Judges to lead the people, when His true desire was to have kings [[8]a type of the apostolic], over them. And when the judge followed the Lord, they did what was right and when he did not; follow the Lord, all manners of wrongdoing followed. There was no internal self-government formed in the people.

The *"Fortress Church"* will be a true *"Fathering Church"* with an Elijah spirit, where the hearts of the fathers have truly been turned to the children and the heart of the children turned to their fathers; resulting in true "Generational Blessings."

The Return Of The Elijah Spirit!
In the Book of Malachi, which was the last documented speaking of God until the birth of Jesus over Four Hundred years later, we see Him placing great emphasis on purity and righteousness. All this cleansing was to take place before the coming of Jesus and it was two fold in nature. While we know that John the Baptist fulfilled the role of being the forerunner to Jesus Christ [for he came in the spirit and power of Elijah], we also know that there is a dimension to the fulfilment of that prophetic word which is still to come.

The following passages of Scripture will assist in bringing greater clarity to this. First we read: Matthew 17:1-13

---

[8] For more on this you can read the author's book "Five Pillars of the Apostolic – Ordering details at the end of this book.

"Now after six days Jesus took Peter, James, and John his brother, led them up on a high mountain by themselves; and He was transfigured before them. His face shone like the sun, and His clothes became as white as the light. And behold, Moses and Elijah appeared to them, talking with Him. Then Peter answered and said to Jesus, "Lord, it is good for us to be here; if You wish, let us make here three tabernacles: one for You, one for Moses, and one for Elijah." While he was still speaking, behold, a bright cloud overshadowed them; and suddenly a voice came out of the cloud, saying, "This is My beloved Son, in whom I am well pleased. Hear Him!" And when the disciples heard it, they fell on their faces and were greatly afraid. But Jesus came and touched them and said, "Arise, and do not be afraid." When they had lifted up their eyes, they saw no one but Jesus only. Now as they came down from the mountain, Jesus commanded them, saying, "Tell the vision to no one until the Son of Man is risen from the dead." And His disciples asked Him, saying, "Why then do the scribes say that Elijah must come first?" Jesus answered and said to them, *Indeed, Elijah is coming first and will restore all things. But I say to you that Elijah has come already*, and they did not know him but did to him whatever they wished. Likewise the Son of Man is also about to suffer at their hands." Then the disciples understood that He spoke to them of John the Baptist." [Italics Added]

In the preceding text we read some very important statements by Jesus, especially verses 11-13 when He declared that Elijah is coming!

Next We Read: John 1:19-28
"Now this is the testimony of John, when the Jews

sent priests and Levites from Jerusalem to ask him, "Who are you?" He confessed, and did not deny, but confessed, "I am not the Christ." And they asked him, "What then? Are you Elijah?" He said, "I am not." "Are you the Prophet?" And he answered, "No." Then they said to him, "Who are you, that we may give an answer to those who sent us? What do you say about yourself?" He said: "I am 'The voice of one crying in the wilderness: "Make straight the way of the LORD," 'as the Prophet Isaiah said." Now those who were sent were from the Pharisees. And they asked him, saying, "Why then do you baptize if you are not the Christ, nor Elijah, nor the Prophet?" John answered them, saying, "I baptize with water, but there stands One among you whom you do not know. It is He who, coming after me, is preferred before me, whose sandal strap I am not worthy to loose." These things were done in Bethabara beyond the Jordan, where John was baptizing."

Here we note the accurate testimony of John concerning himself as he made some very pertinent statements and declared – that he was not Elijah!

John's Ministry

"But the angel said to him, "Do not be afraid, Zacharias, for your prayer is heard; and your wife Elizabeth will bear you a son, and you shall call his name John. And you will have joy and gladness, and many will rejoice at his birth. For he will be great in the sight of the Lord, and shall drink neither wine nor strong drink. He will also be filled with the Holy Spirit, even from his mother's womb. *And he will turn many of the children of Israel to the Lord their God. He will also go before Him in the spirit and power of*

> *Elijah, 'to turn the hearts of the fathers to the children,' and the disobedient to the wisdom of the just, to make ready a people prepared for the Lord."* [Luke 1:13-17 Italics Added]

> "When the messengers of John had departed, He began to speak to the multitudes concerning John: "What did you go out into the wilderness to see? A reed shaken by the wind? But what did you go out to see? A man clothed in soft garments? Indeed those who are gorgeously apparelled and live in luxury are in kings' courts. But what did you go out to see? *A Prophet? Yes, I say to you, and more than a Prophet. This is he of whom it is written: 'Behold, I send My messenger before Your face, who will prepare Your way before You.'"* [Luke 7:24-27 Italics Added]

As we press further into the purposes of the Lord, I would like us to re-visit the ministry of John the Baptist, as this is most relevant to the times in which we live.

To fully understand our ministry in these *"days"*, it is imperative that we understand the ministry of John as he functioned in a similar role to us, the Church in this hour. Most people have come to accept John as a Prophet who walked and functioned in the "spirit and power of Elijah" and this is partly true. However, as Jesus spoke about John before his death, Jesus declared that John was more [not better] than a Prophet. I submit to you that Jesus was speaking about an apostolic dimension operating in John's life. The Church of Jesus Christ is built upon the foundation of the Apostles and Prophets with Jesus Christ being the Chief Cornerstone. The apostolic and prophetic was and still is an inseparable ministry in the Church of Jesus Christ.

Malachi prophesied of the coming of Elijah the Prophet before the final coming of Jesus. However, there is a two-fold fulfilment to this prophetic word. John the Baptist fulfilled the first, and the Mature Church is fulfilling the second.

The prophetic anointing releases the ability to see events in the future and to foretell them. The apostolic anointing has the ability to bring to pass what the prophetic sees. The apostolic anointing says, [9]"This is that which was spoken by the Prophets"

Let us briefly look at five things the apostolic\prophetic anointing caused that was resident in John the Baptist and that is valuable to us as we continue preparing the way of the Lord in this region and in the nations of the earth.

1: *Many Will Rejoice At His Birth:*
John's [10]birth caused many to rejoice because he signalled a new mentality to Kingdom activity, which was [11]Kingdom violence. He was able to bring forth the manifestation of the [12]words prophesied by the law and the Prophets. He also brought joy to many because he declared the Messiah to them.

2: *He Did Not Drink Wine Nor Strong Drink:*
Wine is a mocker of the true anointing and strong drink causes us to forget the law—that is self-government! [13]John was truly a man of internal self-government and that caused him to be intensely focused. This is a reflection of the [14]Nazirite vow, which was accompanied by the fact that no razor was to come upon the head. Hair represents authority,

---

[9] Acts 2:16
[10] Luke 1:14
[11] Matthew 11:12
[12] Matthew 11:13
[13] Luke 1:15
[14] Numbers 6:1-8

and hair being cut was a sign of one's authority being severed. Ergo, this apostolic/prophetic anointing that is being released today will move into a stronger place of self-government and authority in the things of the Spirit.

3: *Filled With The Spirit Of The Lord:*
[15]This is powerful, as it is a higher dimension than that of earthly fathering or mentoring. This is the realm of divine impartation, fathering and release. John's father, Zacharias, could not father or mentor him in order to release him into what God had ordained for him to accomplish – [Zacharias was in unbelief and functioned under an old order which was about to change with the ministry of his son John]. Therefore God Himself, had to mentor and train John. This is what gave him the power and anointing to function the way he did and released him to be able to identify the Christ – Our Saviour and Lord! There is a dimension of the revelation of Christ that the Lord is bringing forth through the apostolic\prophetic that is designed to turn many to the Lord. There is going to be a new release in the evangelistic realm because of the release of this apostolic\prophetic anointing.

4: *The Power To Turn The Hearts Of Fathers, Children And The Disobedient:*[16]
An awesome anointing for impartation and wisdom is released through this apostolic\prophetic anointing. There is also the ability to release true fatherhood from a position of strength and purity.

5: *To Make A People Prepared For The Lord:*[17]
There is a finishing anointing that is also released through this apostolic\prophetic anointing that is being released in

---

[15] Luke 1:15
[16] Luke 1:17
[17] Luke 1:17

this hour. The final product will be a people who are absolutely ready for the return of the Lord.

Remember Malachi prophesied that before the final coming of Jesus that the spirit of Elijah would return. Some may want to argue that Malachi prophesied about John the Baptist. However, as we said before Malachi's prophesy is two-fold; Elijah has come and Elijah is to come!

If we look closer at the actual time that Malachi's prophetic word was to be accomplished, we would see that he places its fulfilment at the end of the age, before the final return of Jesus. We read in Malachi 4:5

> "Behold, I will send you Elijah the Prophet *Before the coming of the great and dreadful day of the Lord.*" [Italics Added]

This had to be referring to the final coming of Jesus because His first coming was not a great and dreadful day. It was a day of deliverance and salvation.

Further Clarity
An amazing event took place in the life of Jesus that will bring absolute clarity to this prophetic word and the relevance it has to the current move of God.

Jesus was about to begin His earthly ministry and after His cousin John baptized Him, was led away into the wilderness to be tested by the devil. After forty days and nights of rigorous prayer and fasting, He defeats the devil and immediately steps into His public ministry. He went to Galilee and the surrounding cities and preached. Evidently, He was well received in those regions.[18]

After His ministry in those regions He returned to Nazareth, His hometown, and as was His custom He went into the synagogue and stood up to read and was handed the Book of the Prophet Isaiah and He read:

> "The Spirit of the LORD is upon Me, Because He has anointed Me *To preach the gospel to the poor; He has sent Me to heal the broken-hearted, To proclaim liberty to the captives And recovery of sight to the blind, To set at liberty those who are oppressed; To proclaim the acceptable year of the LORD." Then He closed the book, and gave it back to the attendant and sat down.* And the eyes of all who were in the synagogue were fixed on Him. And He began to say to them, "Today this Scripture is fulfilled in your hearing" What an incredible moment that must have been, all eyes were fixed on Jesus as He read and then made that proclamation. I mean this is the hometown boy. Not only that, but news travelled fast even in those days [without all the amenities of modern science, World Wide Web included] of His exploits in the surrounded cities, especially Capernaum. [Luke 4:18-22 Italics and Parenthesis Added]

However, let us take a closer look at the text of Scripture that Jesus quoted from, and see the incredible implications of His actions. Jesus was quoting from the Book of Isaiah:

> "The Spirit of the Lord GOD is upon Me, Because the LORD has anointed Me To preach good tidings to the

---

[18] Luke 4:13-15

poor; He has sent Me to heal the broken-hearted, To proclaim liberty to the captives, And the opening of the prison to those who are bound; To proclaim the acceptable year of the LORD, *And the day of vengeance of our God*..." [Isaiah 61:1-2 Italics Added]

As can be noticed, Jesus ends His reading right in the middle of a sentence. Well, what is the implication of this, one may ask?

The Implication Is!
Jesus' first entrance upon planet earth was not to bring judgment, but Salvation [for that's what His name meant – Matthew 1:21 "And she will bring forth a Son, and you shall call His name Jesus, for He will save His people from their sins."]. This is why He stopped His apostolic decree right in the middle of the sentence. This takes us even further into another line of questioning – who will proclaim the day of vengeance of our God? The answer can only be – We the Church – Jesus' Body!

In the light of this we can now see and understand that Malachi was truly speaking about the days preceding the last advent of Jesus. When He comes the final time He will not be coming to save the people from their sins, but He will come as King and Judge!

Preparing The Way:
As it was with Jesus' first coming so shall it be with His final coming. John the Baptist preceded Him, walking in the spirit and power of Elijah "preparing the way" before Him:

"In those days John the Baptist came preaching in the wilderness of Judea, and saying, "Repent, for the kingdom of heaven is at hand!" For this is he who was spoken of by the Prophet Isaiah, saying: "The voice of one crying in the wilderness: *'Prepare the way of the LORD; Make His paths straight.'"* [Matthew 3:1-3 Italics Added]

Just before John's birth, the Angel of the Lord appeared to his father Zacharias and proclaimed:

"Then an angel of the Lord appeared to him, standing on the right side of the altar of incense. And when Zacharias saw him, he was troubled, and fear fell upon him. But the angel said to him, "Do not be afraid, Zacharias, for your prayer is heard; and your wife Elizabeth will bear you a son, and you shall call his name John. And you will have joy and gladness, and many will rejoice at his birth. For he will be great in the sight of the Lord, and shall drink neither wine nor strong drink. He will also be filled with the Holy Spirit, even from his mother's womb. *And he will turn many of the children of Israel to the Lord their God. He will also go before Him in the spirit and power of Elijah, 'to turn the hearts of the fathers to the children,' and the disobedient to the wisdom of the just, to make ready a people prepared for the Lord."* [Luke 1:11-17 Italics Added]

In like manner there must be a people in the earth who can and must *"prepare the way"* for the final coming of Jesus.

They must also walk in the spirit and power of Elijah, to turn the hearts of the fathers to the children, and the disobedient to the wisdom of the just, to make ready a people prepared for the Lord. If you can receive it I submit to you that the [19]apostolic/prophetic restoration that is now taking place in

---

[19] You can read the author's book "Five Pillars of The Apostolic" for a more in-depth analysis on the restorations of Apostles.

the Body of Christ is being released in the same spirit and power of Elijah. There is such an awesome anointing being released into the Body of Christ for uncompromising function in the will of God. In every nation, in every jurisdiction, men and women of God are beginning to forsake the error of their ways, repenting and renouncing sinful practices and crying out for the move of God's Spirit as never before. I tell you, God has already begun to respond, and *"purity"* is the buzzword in the spirit realm and in the heart of all of God's true Apostles!

The Spirit And Power Of Elijah:
To gain full understanding of what the spirit of Elijah is, we must examine Elijah's life and re-visit Mt. Carmel[20]. He single-handedly challenged and defeated four hundred and fifty false prophets of Baal upon Mt. Carmel. This was the site of Elijah's confrontation and destruction of the four hundred and fifty false prophets of Baal. [We will look deeper into this "one man" in a later section.] This single event exacted such change that Israel turned back to God and also revealed the power and glory of God to the people.

As we read the life of this great man of God we realize that everything that happened in his life was training for his Mt. Carmel experience. God raised him up to change an apostate nation by aggressively warring against and dismantling the powers of darkness over the nation.

Some of the legitimate questions that can be asked concerning this awesome prophet of God are – what was the operating system of this man's life? What made him function the way that he did? Was he endowed with some kind of special anointing that we can never posses? And the list can go on;

---

[20] 1 Kings Chapters 17 and 18

however we want to look a bit deeper into the life of this major Prophet of God and see the foundation of his life.

He Was A Man Of Purity; Living A Sanctified Life:
This is reflected; by the very first thing that he did when he called the people to make a choice between Baal and God:

> "Then it happened, when Ahab saw Elijah, that Ahab said to him, "Is that you, O troubler of Israel?" And he answered, "I have not troubled Israel, but you and your father's house have, in that you have forsaken the commandments of the LORD and you have followed the Baals. Now therefore, send and gather all Israel to me on Mount Carmel, the four hundred and fifty Prophets of Baal, and the four hundred Prophets of Asherah, who eat at Jezebel's table." So Ahab sent for all the children of Israel, and gathered the Prophets together on Mount Carmel. *And Elijah came to all the people, and said, "How long will you falter between two opinions? If the LORD is God, follow Him; but if Baal, follow him."* But the people answered him not a word." [1 Kings 18:17-21 Italics Added]

The spirit and power of Elijah goes against complacency and worldliness. It confronts the religious spirit that makes people hearers of the Word and not doers. It attacks the very demonic power that causes the "*Word of God to be ineffective*"

> "Then the Pharisees and scribes asked Him, "Why do Your disciples not walk according to the tradition of the elders, but eat bread with unwashed hands?" He answered and said to them, "Well did Isaiah prophesy of you hypocrites, as it is written: 'This people honours Me with their lips, But their heart is far from Me. And in vain they worship Me, Teaching as doctrines the

commandments of men.' "For laying aside the commandment of God, you hold the tradition of men -the washing of pitchers and cups, and many other such things you do." And He said to them, "All too well you reject the commandment of God, that you may keep your tradition. For Moses said, 'Honour your father and your mother'; and, 'He who curses father or mother, let him be put to death.' But you say, 'If a man says to his father or mother, "Whatever profit you might have received from me is Corban"--' [that is, a gift to God], then you no longer let him do anything for his father or his mother, *making the word of God of no effect through your tradition which you have handed down.* And many such things you do." [Mark 7:5-13 Italics Added]

It also attacks that spirit that causes one to have a "form of godliness, but denying the power thereof" – [2 Timothy 3:5]. It draws a line between the holy and the profane and pushes people to a place of sanctification, purity and unswerving commitment to the Lord.

This was also reflected in him restoring the Altars of the Lord – the true, pure places of worship.

> "And he repaired the altar of the LORD that was broken down. And Elijah took twelve stones, according to the number of the tribes of the sons of Jacob, to whom the word of the LORD had come, saying, "Israel shall be your name." Then with the stones he built an altar in the name of the LORD" [1 Kings 18:30-32]

Altars represent places of sacrifice, purity, sanctification and true commitment! The Elijah spirit always pushes the follower of God to return to the Altar.

> "In those days John the Baptist came preaching in the wilderness of Judea, and saying, *"Repent, for the kingdom of heaven is at hand!"* For this is he who was spoken of by the Prophet Isaiah, saying: "The voice of one crying in the wilderness: *'Prepare the way of the LORD; Make His paths straight.'*" [Matthew 3:1-3 Italics Added]

> "I beseech you therefore, brethren, by the mercies of God, that *you present your bodies a living sacrifice, holy, acceptable to God, which is your reasonable service.* And *do not be conformed to this world, but be transformed by the renewing of your mind*, that you may prove what is that good and acceptable and perfect will of God." [Romans 12:1-2 Italics Added]

Elijah restores the Altar and then goes on to prepare the sacrifice. Through the apostolic restoration that is taking place we are beginning to see pure worship restored, pure communion restored as well as pure commitment restored to the People of God. There is a new breed of Christians arising in the earth that will not compromise and will walk in purity!

He Was A True Leader:
> "Now therefore, send and gather all Israel to me on Mount Carmel, the four hundred and fifty Prophets of Baal, and the four hundred Prophets of Asherah, who eat at Jezebel's table... Then Elijah said to all the people, *"Come near to me." So all the people came near to him."* [1 Kings 18:19, 30 Italics Added]

This is the heart of a true leader. He does not send people away in their confusion and sin, but seeks to draw them near. Elijah did not consider himself to be the only righteous man in Israel, nor the man of God for the hour. He did not cast judgment upon those who were not walking accurately in the things of God. Instead of judgment and washing his hands of them, he lays his life on the line for the People of God and presents true leadership to them. He identifies with the people and restores the true Government of God in their lives.

The true Elijah/prophetic anointing is aggressive and confrontational but it operates from a heart that loves people. It wants to confront people with the view of bringing them closer to God.

He Was A Man That Knew How To Draw Near To God:
"And it came to pass, at the time of the offering of the evening sacrifice, that Elijah the Prophet came near and said, "LORD God of Abraham, Isaac, and Israel, let it be known this day that You are God in Israel and I am Your servant, and that I have done all these things at Your word. Hear me, O LORD, hear me, that this people may know that You are the LORD God, and that You have turned their hearts back to You again." Then the fire of the LORD fell and consumed the burnt sacrifice, and the wood and the stones and the dust, and it licked up the water that was in the trench. Now when all the people saw it, they fell on their faces; and they said, "The LORD, He is God! The LORD, He is God!" [1 Kings 18:36-39]

Verse 36 gives us the key to unlock the door to the Power of God! At the time of the evening sacrifice Elijah draws near to God!

This is awesome, for as we draw near to God we cannot help but be pure and holy and this releases the Lord to do great and mighty things through us. For the Word of God says that as we "draw near to God, He will draw near to us"[21] and when this happens cleansing and purification take place, resulting in the Lord elevating us.

> "*Draw near to God and He will draw near to you.* Cleanse your hands, you sinners; and purify your hearts, you double-minded. Lament and mourn and weep! Let your laughter be turned to mourning and your joy to gloom. Humble yourselves in the sight of the Lord, and He will lift you up." [James 4:8-10 Italics Added]

We are not called to pray empty prayers that cannot cause breakthrough! We are called to prayer with strength, wisdom and intensity.

Elijah's Prayer:
He addresses a patriarchal God! "Lord God of Abraham, Isaac and Israel…" [1 Kings 18:36] He knows that God has worked throughout the generations and can work in his generation as well. He goes on to pray – let it be known this day! Not in somebody else's day! Today, in our day! Oh! I tell you, this is part of the *"apostolic grace"*, and it has the ability to bring things into the present reality, into what the Spirit of God is currently speaking to the Church! – It loves to bring clarity! It loves to say, "This is that which was spoken."[22]

Remember the Word of God declares to us that Elijah was a man with a nature like ours – James 5:17-18!

> "*Elijah was a man with a nature like ours*, and he prayed earnestly that it would not rain; and it did not

---

[21] James 4:8-10
[22] Acts 2:16

rain on the land for three years and six months. And he prayed again, and the heaven gave rain, and the earth produced its fruit." [Italics Added]

He was very much a human being who flowed and functioned in a crazy mixed up world just like ours and he had to confront and deal with the issues of his day. Much like us, he had his areas of shortcomings but God worked through his life. Likewise God can work through our lives as we surrender our all on the Altar for Him.

Pitfalls Of The Elijah Spirit
It is vital that we look at some of the pitfalls we need to avoid, with this prophetic anointing. Elijah moved from the mountaintop of victory to the abyss of defeat and death[23], and we need to uncover the reason, so as to avoid making the same errors. As the Word of God declares to us that:

> *"All Scripture is given by inspiration of God, and is profitable for doctrine, for reproof, for correction, for instruction in righteousness,* that the man of God may be complete, thoroughly equipped for every good work." [2 Timothy 3:16-17 Italics Added]

Hence we need to examine Elijah's life from a microscopic viewpoint.

One Man!
Elijah became so engulfed in his own significance and walk that he thought he was the only man alive that was walking accurately in the Will of God! Herein lies one of the greatest traps of the Elijah spirit that we need to avoid in this apostolic and prophetic restoration.

---

[23] 1 Kings 19:4

> "*And there he went into a cave*, and spent the night in that place; and behold, the word of the LORD came to him, and He said to him, "What are you doing here, Elijah?" So he said, "I have been very zealous for the LORD God of hosts; for the children of Israel have forsaken Your covenant, torn down Your altars, and killed Your Prophets with the sword. *I alone am left*; and they seek to take my life." [1 Kings 19:9-10 Italics Added]

God's Response!
> "Yet *I have reserved seven thousand* in Israel, *all whose knees have not bowed to Baal*, and every mouth that has not kissed him." 1 Kings 19:18 [Italics added]

God was saying to him, "*listen Elijah, do not even think that it was your "one man"* heroics that accomplished these mighty acts. I want you to understand that there were Seven Thousand others that were ready to accomplish mighty and awesome exploits for Me. Elijah you were only the "spearhead" but I had a shaft of "Seven Thousand" attached to you which would assist in accomplishing the task. Elijah's tenure on earth did not last much past the unhealthy mindset of him being the only one that was standing for God. The Lord appears to him in 1 Kings Chapter 19 and declares the end of his tenure:

> "Then the LORD said to him: "Go, return on your way to the Wilderness of Damascus; and when you arrive, anoint Hazael as king over Syria. Also you shall anoint Jehu the son of Nimshi as king over Israel. And Elisha the son of Shaphat of Abel Meholah you shall anoint as prophet in your place." [1 Kings 19:15-16]

The outcome of the directive saw Elijah being taken of the scene and Elisha stepping into his prophetic word and function.

So many churches and ministries today have the same mindset as Elijah and believe that they are the only ones doing the Will of God. Some ministries hold *"centre stage"* and they assume that they are the only right ones favoured by God.

Let me share with you an imagery the Lord gave me recently. He showed me a city and in that city there were several containers of varying sizes all filled with seawater. Then He showed me the ocean and said to me that it represented His Kingdom, and then proceeded to explain an interesting scenario. He said if you were to test the water in each of the containers, it would produce the exact same results as that of the ocean. He said therein lies the problem with most churches. They assume that, because they consist of the same composition as that of the Kingdom, they are the "church or ministry" in that nation. They call themselves "the territorial church" of that region or nation.

The Lord continued saying to me that the high esteem these churches have for themselves is akin to thinking that any one of the containers that was filled with seawater was the ocean. The point is that no matter how much you think you as an individual are serving God, He always has a "seven thousand" walking in His Will and creating the necessary openings and breakthroughs for "Elijah" to be successful in establishing God's ordained Will. I hope you get the point! It is time for churches and ministries in every nation to really wise up and get the message – we are all in this together, and it is time to place all on the Altar and walk in purity, righteousness, and holiness as well as in the bond of peace and in unison in order to get the job done. I know it is easier said than done, but God by His Holy Spirit is releasing an anointing in this hour for it to be accomplished.

After Elijah slew the prophets of Baal for God the enemy did just what he does to every one of us after a resounding victory over his domain. He tries to negate the impact, by causing us to turn our attention away from the Lord and His voice, to our importance and significance in the working of God. This is what happened as soon as Elijah destroyed the 450 false prophets of Baal. His actions caused an awesome victory to come to the people of God and returned them to the realm of purity. The devil stirred up Jezebel and she declared:

> "Then Jezebel sent a messenger to Elijah, saying, "So let the gods do to me, and more also, if I do not make your life as the life of one of them by tomorrow about this time." [1 Kings 19:2]

As we read on in the Chapter we see that Elijah fled in an attempt to save his life and fell from a mountaintop of victory to the abyss of defeat and death – He just came down from Mt. Carmel where he had birthed another mighty move of God in prayer to a place where he was fleeing for his life and wishing he could die. He entered into a season of self-pity.

> *"And when he saw that, he arose and ran for his life*, and went to Beersheba, which belongs to Judah, and left his servant there. But he himself went a day's journey into the wilderness, and came and sat down under a broom tree. And he prayed that he might die, and said, "It is enough! *Now, LORD, take my life, for I am no better than my fathers!"* [1 Kings 19:3-4 Italics Added]

Built for the
GLORY OF GOD

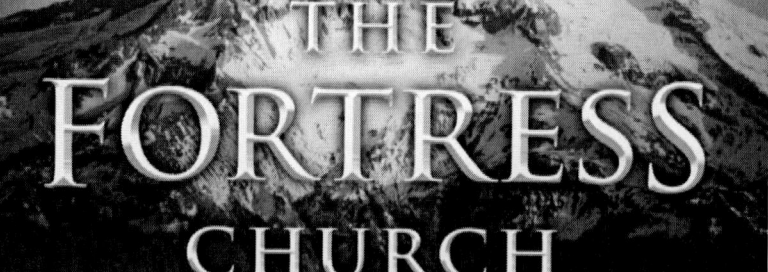

THE FORTRESS CHURCH

MICHAEL SCANTLEBURY

☞ CHAPTER 3

PROPHETIC ISAIAH'S VIEW

Another dimension of this *"Fortress Church"* is the grace anointing from the Lord, to bring in the Harvest. This *"Fortress Church"* is also spoken of in the Book of Isaiah:

> "The word that Isaiah the son of Amoz saw concerning Judah and Jerusalem. *Now it shall come to pass in the latter days That the mountain of the LORD's house Shall be established on the top of the mountains, And shall be exalted above the hills; And all nations shall flow to it.* Many people shall come and say, "Come, and let us go up to the mountain of the LORD, To the house of the God of Jacob; He will teach us His ways, And we shall walk in His paths." *For out of Zion shall go forth the law, And the word of the LORD from Jerusalem.* He shall judge between the nations, And rebuke many people; They shall beat their swords into ploughshares, And their spears into pruning hooks; Nation shall not lift up sword against nation, Neither shall they learn war anymore."
> [Isaiah 2:1-4 Italics Added]

This is so awesome! The Prophet Isaiah is given this panoramic view of the *Fortress Church* and it is so very powerful.

We would all agree that Isaiah is indeed speaking about the Church, the Lord's House, or Zion if you will of that there should be no doubt.

As it was stated earlier, the *Fortress Church* will be in an elevated position, her status of being "seated in heavenly places in Christ Jesus" will be accentuated in these times.

Contrary to some popular opinions, the Church that is emerging in this hour will see the nations coming to Her for guidance. This is already occurring in some quarters as leaders of nations seek out the counsel of godly men. This Church is described as *established and exalted*. This is the mandate upon the "Five-Fold" ministry, to bring the Church of the Living God to a place of ordained strength and maturity. I love how the Apostle Paul declares it in the following passage:

> "Now to Him who is able to establish you according to my gospel and the preaching of Jesus Christ, *according to the revelation of the mystery kept secret since the world began but now has been made manifest, and by the prophetic Scriptures has been made known to all nations*, according to the commandment of the everlasting God, for obedience to the faith - to God, alone wise, be glory through Jesus Christ forever. Amen." [Romans 16:25-27 Italics Added]

The Prophet goes on to declare that the law will proceed out of Zion. The law here is not referring to legalism but instead it is referring to lifestyle principles. This *"Fortress Church"* will be a place where the Saints will be walking in "Lifestyle Christianity", not Sunday morning theatrics. They will demonstrate the quality of life for which our Lord Jesus Christ purchased with His Blood.

However, there is something of tremendous note that occurs in this *"latter days,"* *"Fortress Church,"* a command goes forth for them to beat their swords into ploughshares, and their spears into pruning hooks. This is powerful for two reasons as it implies the following:

Firstly, in order for the Church to get to the place of being established on top of the mountain, she had to war her way to it. She arrived at the top of the mountain with sword and spear in hand. This is why the church today must have fully functioning *"true Apostles"* within her if we are to arrive at this pre-determined destination of ruling among the nations. I believe that many *"false apostles"* will be exposed in this hour!

I believe that many *"true, and proven Apostles"* are being released/made manifest by the Lord in this hour, to sharpen us in understanding His Will and Purpose. Knowledge is power, which is why Daniel declared:

> *"Those who do wickedly against the covenant he shall corrupt with flattery; but the people who know their God shall be strong, and carry out great exploits. And those of the people who understand shall instruct many..."* [Daniel 11:32-33 Italicized]

I believe that these *"true Apostles"* are being used by the Lord to sharpen the Saints. Remember, we the Saints are the Lord's Battleaxes. We are the ones He uses in accomplishing His will. As we are sharpened in our understanding of Him and His perfect will, we can then execute His written judgements. There is a massive warfare for the minds of men. The mind is the biggest and greatest battleground, for the Word of God declares "For as he thinks in his heart, so is he." [Proverbs 23:6]

The Apostle Paul also describes it this way:
> "For the weapons of our warfare are not carnal but mighty in God for *pulling down strongholds, casting*

down arguments and every high thing that exalts itself against the knowledge of God, bringing every thought into captivity to the obedience of Christ, and being ready to punish all disobedience when your obedience is fulfilled." [2 Corinthians 10:4-6 Italics Added]

He clearly shows us that the battle is in the thought realm. Hence, part of the mandate given to the Apostles in this hour is to destroy wrong mindsets, concepts and principles that have been established in the minds of the Saints, and replace them with correct ones.

Secondly, when this is accomplished, we are going to see one of the largest harvests of souls the world has ever seen. The command goes forth for the Saints to beat their swords into ploughshares, And their spears into pruning hooks. Their weapons of warfare are now returned to farming implements; which will be used in the greatest harvest of the ages.

The Blacksmiths:
> *"You are My battle-axe and weapons of war:* For with you I will break the nation in pieces; With you I will destroy kingdoms; With you I will break in pieces the horse and its rider; With you I will break in pieces the chariot and its rider; With you also I will break in pieces man and woman; With you I will break in pieces old and young; With you I will break in pieces the young man and the maiden; With you also I will break in pieces the shepherd and his flock; With you I will break in pieces the farmer and his yoke of oxen; And with you I will break in pieces governors and rulers. "And I will repay Babylon And all the inhabitants of Chaldea For all the evil they have done In Zion in your sight," says the LORD." [Jeremiah 51:20-24 Italics Added]

Today Blacksmiths [Apostles] are the *"Revelators"* of God's

Word who are being used to assist in building the Church of Christ. They are the Apostles that are being raised up in every nation, proclaiming that we are in the midst of yet another *"reformation"* after that of [24]Martin Luther! They are the ones the Lord is using to help in [25]sharpening and [26]perfecting the Saints for the work of the ministry:

I declare to you that in many quarters there are no Blacksmiths [Apostles] who can sharpen the Saints' – God's weapons of warfare. Let us, as we continue our press, stay connected to the Blacksmiths that the Lord has given to us. Remember, [27]the weapons of our warfare are not carnal but mighty in God to the pulling down of every stronghold, and every high thing that seeks to exalt itself against the knowledge of God. Remember that the Word of God declares that we [the Saints] are God's battle-axes:

> *"You are My battle-ax and weapons of war*: For with you I will break the nation in pieces; With you I will destroy kingdoms; With you I will break in pieces the horse and its rider; With you I will break in pieces the chariot and its rider; With you also I will break in pieces man and woman; With you I will break in pieces old and young; With you I will break in pieces the young man and the maiden; With you also I will break in pieces the shepherd and his flock; With you I will break in pieces the farmer and his yoke of oxen; And with you I will break in pieces governors and rulers. "And I will repay Babylon And all the inhabitants of Chaldea For all the evil they have done

---

[24] He was the great German priest who began the great reformation and began what is called the "Protestant Movement"
[25] Proverbs 27:17
[26] Ephesians 4:11-12
[27] 2 Corinthians 10:3-6

In Zion in your sight," says the LORD." [Jeremiah 51:20-24 Italics Added]

Quite apart from working to refine metals and hammering them into shape, Blacksmiths/Apostles are also to sharpen weapons of war for battle.

This is why it is absolutely necessary for Apostles to be accepted by the Body of Christ, and allowed to mature and function so that we can all be helped in being [28]equipped to do the work of the ministry.

[29]Destroying Babylon
Babylon has always sought to come against the things and people of God. In ancient times it moved against the Israelites and destroyed Jerusalem and took the best and brightest of its young citizens from the tribe of Judah to serve its evil schemes. There was a young man named Daniel along with his three friends Hananiah, Mishael, and Azariah that were forced into Babylon. These four young men represented a vision of the Fortress Church. They fought against Babylon's system and won.

The Daniel Example
Daniel is a tremendous apostolic figure in the Scriptures. King Nebuchadnezzar of Babylon, besieged Jerusalem, destroyed it, and took the best and the brightest to influence and strengthen his domain. His kingdom was very expansive; it covered most of the then Middle East. Daniel was taken along with his three friends and incarcerated in Babylon. He was between the age of 13-16 years and the 12

---

[28] Ephesians 4:12
[29] Extract taken from the author's book "Five Pillars of The Apostolic" as he thought it very vital and relevant to this writing!

Chapters of the Book of Daniel span over a 65-year period. He stood as a strong and influential figure, under four successive kings, and two successive kingdoms, Babylon and Medo-Persia and remained relevant in every change.

Please understand that Daniel was initially trained in Israel. In fact, his formative years had already passed, and Babylon [a type of the religious, political, social, economic system of the world], wanted to have these boys for its use.

Even though Daniel was trained in the [30]language and literature of Babylon, it was God who gave him the wisdom to [31]function successfully in Babylon.

> "As for these four young men, God gave them knowledge and skill in all literature and wisdom; and Daniel had understanding in all visions and dreams." [Daniel 1:17]

> *"There is a man in your kingdom in whom is the Spirit of the Holy God. And in the days of your father, light and understanding and wisdom, like the wisdom of the gods, were found in him*; and king Nebuchadnezzar your father -your father the king- made him chief of the magicians, astrologers, Chaldeans, and soothsayers. *Inasmuch as an excellent spirit, knowledge, under-standing, interpreting dreams, solving riddles, and explaining enigmas were found in this Daniel* whom the king named Belteshazzar, now let Daniel be called and he will give the interpretation." [Daniel 5:11-12 Italics Added]

Daniel did not rely upon the "wisdom" of the Babylonians to function; he totally relied upon God's wisdom. In fact, it is

---

[30] Daniel 1:4
[31] Daniel 1:17 & Daniel 5:11

very interesting to note the issue, surrounding Daniel's initial promotion. King Nebuchadnezzar had a dream that he could not remember, let alone have interpreted.

> "Now in the second year of Nebuchadnezzar's reign, Nebuchadnezzar had dreams, and his spirit was so troubled that his sleep left him. Then the king gave the command to call the magicians, the astrologers, the sorcerers, and the Chaldeans to tell the king his dreams. So they came and stood before the king. And the king said to them, 'I have had a dream, and my spirit is anxious to know the dream.' Then the Chaldeans spoke to the king in Aramaic, 'O king, live forever! Tell your servants the dream, and we will give the interpretation.' The king answered and said to the Chaldeans, 'My decision is firm: If you do not make known the dream to me, and its interpretation, you shall be cut in pieces, and your houses shall be made an ash heap. 'However, if you tell the dream and its interpretation, you shall receive from me gifts, rewards, and great honour. Therefore tell me the dream and its interpretation.' They answered again and said, 'Let the king tell his servants the dream and we will give its interpretation.' The king answered and said, 'know for certain that you would gain time, because you see that my decision is firm: 'If you do not make known the dream to me, there is only one decree for you! For you have agreed to speak lying and corrupt words before me till the time has changed. Therefore tell me the dream, and I shall know that you can give me its interpretation.' The Chaldeans answered the king, and said: 'There is not a man on earth who can tell the king's matter; therefore no king, lord, or ruler has ever asked such things of any magician, astrologer, or Chaldean.'" [Daniel 2:1-10]

Of course the Lord had set the whole thing up, and there was no one in the demonic realm that could interpret the king's dream. demonic powers and principalities do not have a clue as to what the Lord is doing. They do not posses the wisdom that God has, and it is always sad when the People of God rely on "earthly wisdom" to accomplish spiritual things.

As the [32]decree goes out, and all the wise men are being sought after and killed, Daniel steps up and declares Godly wisdom, far beyond anything Babylon had ever seen:

> "*Then with counsel and wisdom Daniel answered* Arioch, the captain of the king's guard, who had gone out to kill the wise men of Babylon; He answered and said to Arioch the king's captain, 'Why is the decree from the king so urgent?' Then Arioch made the decision known to Daniel. So Daniel went in and asked the king to give him time, that he might tell the king the interpretation. *Then Daniel went to his house, and made the decision known to Hananiah, Mishael, and Azariah, his companions, That they might seek mercies from the God of heaven concerning this secret, so that Daniel and his companions might not perish with the rest of the wise men of Babylon. Then the secret was revealed to Daniel in a night vision. So Daniel blessed the God of heaven.* Daniel answered and said: 'Blessed be the name of God forever and ever, For wisdom and might are His. And He changes the times and the seasons; He removes kings and raises up kings; He gives wisdom to the wise and knowledge to those who have understanding. He reveals deep and secret things; He knows what is in

---

[32] Daniel 2:13

> the darkness, And light dwells with Him. I thank You and praise You, O God of my fathers; You have given me wisdom and might, and have now made known to me what we asked of You, for You have made known to us the king's demand.'" ...Then King Nebuchadnezzar fell on his face, prostrate before Daniel, and commanded that they should present an offering and incense to him. The king answered Daniel, and said, *"Truly your God is the God of gods, the Lord of kings, and a revealer of secrets, since you could reveal this secret."* Then the king promoted Daniel and gave him many great gifts; and he made him ruler over the whole province of Babylon, and chief administrator over all the wise men of Babylon. Also Daniel petitioned the king, and he set Shadrach, Meshach, and Abed-nego over the affairs of the province of Babylon; but Daniel sat in the gate of the king. [Daniel 2:14-23; 46-49 Italics Added]

Daniel then goes on to give the dream and its interpretation to king Nebuchadnezzar[33]. It was because this level of wisdom did not exist in all the domain of Babylon, that Daniel was promoted. No one possessed it. The strength of the world had no idea what to do. demonic wisdom was useless at this level.

> "Then king Nebuchadnezzar fell on his face, prostrate before Daniel, and commanded that they should present an offering and incense to him. The king answered Daniel, and said, 'Truly your God is the God of gods, the Lord of kings, and a revealer of secrets, since you could reveal this secret.' *Then the king promoted Daniel and gave him many great gifts; and*

---

[33] Daniel 2:24-45

he made him rule over the whole province of Babylon, and chief administrator over all the wise men of Babylon. Also Daniel petitioned the king and he set Shadrach, Meshach, Abed-Nego over the affairs of the province of Babylon; but Daniel sat in the gate of the king." [Daniel 2:46-49 Italics Added]

With the restoration of the Apostles, this is the dimension of wisdom that is returning to the Church. This level of wisdom is part of the technology that the Lord will use to dismantle and destroy Babylon.

Remember, the Babylonian system still exists in the earth. It is just as alive, just as pernicious, just as expansionist as it was in Daniel's day. Babylon is still seeking a generation that can affect the present and the future.

The word training is also a very interesting Hebrew word. It is the word, Gadal – to become strong! To become valuable! To be powerful! It also defines a continuous, developmental process of growth toward greatness.

So in this context, they were to become strong, to be used in the service of Babylon. We have seen this happen, as a lot of bright young Christians have been drawn away over the decades, into the world system, and used to promote its values. They were "trained by Babylon".

We now need to have strong churches [*Fortress churches*] that can rip people out of Babylon and bring them into the Kingdom of God.

Everything in the world's system is designed to "train or school" us to serve it, and to lose sight of the true realm of the Kingdom of God. It is designed to cause us to become ambivalent to Kingdom values and principles.

We are called to live in this world, but not be a part of its system. We have to live right in the mess, and not be contaminated by it. We must live with the wisdom of God, and have an overcoming nature, to be successful in this present world.

This present Babylonian system will fall; it will be destroyed by the rock cut out the mountain – which represents the Kingdom of God – the Church, the Body of Christ in the earth. We will be used to destroy Babylon. However, this Fortress Church must have Her Blacksmiths/Apostles returned and be fully functioning so that we can be prepared to fulfil this awesome task!

> "This is the dream. Now we will tell the interpretation of it before the king. You, O king, are a king of kings. For the God of heaven has given you a kingdom, power, strength, and glory; and wherever the children of men dwell, or the beasts of the field and the birds of the heaven, He has given them into your hand, and has made you ruler over them all-- you are this head of gold. But after you shall arise another kingdom inferior to yours; then another, a third kingdom of bronze, which shall rule over all the earth. And the fourth kingdom shall be as strong as iron, inasmuch as iron breaks in pieces and shatters everything; and like iron that crushes, that kingdom will break in pieces and crush all the others. Whereas you saw the feet and toes, partly of potter's clay and partly of iron, the kingdom shall be divided; yet the strength of the iron shall be in it, just as you saw the iron mixed with ceramic clay. And as the toes of the feet were partly of iron and partly of clay,

so the kingdom shall be partly strong and partly fragile. As you saw iron mixed with ceramic clay, they will mingle with the seed of men; but they will not adhere to one another, just as iron does not mix with clay. And in the days of these kings the God of heaven will set up a kingdom which shall never be destroyed; and the kingdom shall not be left to other people; it shall break in pieces and consume all these kingdoms, and it shall stand forever. Inasmuch as you saw that the stone was cut out of the mountain without hands, and that it broke in pieces the iron, the bronze, the clay, the silver, and the gold--the great God has made known to the king what will come to pass after this. The dream is certain, and its interpretation is sure." [Daniel 2:36-45]

Isn't it interesting that when Babylon falls, in the Book of Revelation the Lord calls for the Apostles and Prophets to rejoice?

"After these things I saw another angel coming down from heaven, having great authority, and the earth was illuminated with his glory. And he cried mightily with a loud voice, saying, *"Babylon the great is fallen, is fallen, and has become a dwelling place of demons, a prison for every foul spirit, and a cage for every unclean and hated bird!* For all the nations have drunk of the wine of the wrath of her fornication, the kings of the earth have committed fornication with her, and the merchants of the earth have become rich through the abundance of her luxury." And I heard another voice from heaven saying, "Come out of her, my people, lest you share in her sins, and lest you receive of her plagues. For her sins have reached to heaven, and God has remembered her iniquities. *Render to her just as she rendered to you, and repay her double according to her works; in the cup which she has mixed, mix double* for her. In the measure that she glorified herself and lived luxuriously, in the same measure give her torment and sorrow; for she says in her heart, 'I sit as queen, and am no widow, and will not see sorrow.' "Therefore her plagues will come in one day--death and mourning and famine. And she will be utterly burned with fire, for strong is the Lord God who judges her. "The kings of the earth who committed fornication and lived luxuriously with her will weep and lament for her, when they see the smoke of her burning, standing at a distance for fear of her torment, saying, 'Alas, alas, *that great city Babylon, that mighty city! For in one hour your judgment has come.*' "And the merchants of the earth will weep and mourn over her, for no one buys their merchandise anymore: merchandise of gold and silver, precious stones and pearls, fine linen and purple, silk and scarlet, every kind of citron wood, every kind of object of ivory, every kind of object of most precious wood, bronze, iron, and marble; and cinnamon and incense, fragrant oil and frankincense, wine and oil, fine flour and wheat, cattle and sheep, horses and chariots, and bodies and souls of men. The fruit that your soul longed for has gone from you, and all the things which are rich and splendid have gone from you, and you shall find them no more at all. The merchants of these things, who became rich by her, will stand at a distance for fear of her torment, weeping and wailing, and saying, 'Alas, alas, that great city that was clothed in fine linen, purple, and scarlet, and adorned with gold and precious stones and pearls! For in one hour such great riches came to nothing.' Every shipmaster, all who travel by ship, sailors, and as many as trade on the sea, stood at a distance and cried out when they saw the smoke of her burning, saying, 'What is like this great city?' "They threw dust on their heads and cried out, weeping and wailing, and saying, 'Alas, alas, that great city, in which all who had ships on the sea became rich by her wealth! For in one hour she is made desolate.' "*Rejoice over her, O heaven, and you holy apostles and prophets*, for God has avenged you on her!" [Revelation 18:1-20 Italics Added]

However, please understand that the Apostles themselves must go through the refining and hammering process in order to be effectively used by God. One cannot claim "Apostleship" without the due process and resulting evidence. In many quarters some assume that Apostles are the "untouchables" who can touch everyone and everything and bring them, and it, into alignment and shape, without they themselves being touched.

Built for the
GLORY OF GOD

THE
FORTRESS
CHURCH

MICHAEL SCANTLEBURY

☞ CHAPTER 4

THE ANTIOCH CHURCH MODEL

The Antioch Church in the Book of Acts best models this *"Fortress Church"*, and as such we would do well if we explore its operations! Here are a few dynamics of this Antioch Church:

Acts 1:19-26
"Now those who had been scattered by the persecution that broke out when Stephen was killed traveled as far as Phoenicia, Cyprus and Antioch, spreading the word only among Jews. [20] Some of them, however, men from Cyprus and Cyrene, went to Antioch and began to speak to Greeks also, telling them the good news about the Lord Jesus. [21] The Lord's hand was with them, and a great number of people believed and turned to the Lord. [22] News of this reached the church in Jerusalem, and they sent Barnabas to Antioch. [23] When he arrived and saw what the grace of God had done, he was glad and encouraged them all to remain true to the Lord with all their hearts. [24] He was a good man, full of the Holy Spirit and faith, and a great number of people were brought to the Lord. [25] Then Barnabas went to Tarsus to look for Saul, [26] and when he found him, he brought him to Antioch. So for a whole year Barnabas and Saul met with the church and taught great numbers of people. The disciples were called Christians first at Antioch. [27] During this time some prophets came down

prophets came down from Jerusalem to Antioch. ²⁸ One of them, named Agabus, stood up and through the Spirit predicted that a severe famine would spread over the entire Roman world. (This happened during the reign of Claudius.) ²⁹ The disciples, as each one was able, decided to provide help for the brothers and sisters living in Judea. ³⁰ This they did, sending their gift to the elders by Barnabas and Saul."

Acts 13:1-3
"Now in the church at Antioch there were prophets and teachers: Barnabas, Simeon called Niger, Lucius of Cyrene, Manaen [who had been brought up with Herod the tetrarch] and Saul. ² While they were worshiping the Lord and fasting, the Holy Spirit said, "Set apart for me Barnabas and Saul for the work to which I have called them." ³ So after they had fasted and prayed, they placed their hands on them and sent them off."

The Antioch Church Was:
- A multi-ethnic church, since there were several different people groups in it!
- It was a Multi-Cultural Church!
- A place where the rich and poor, educated and uneducated built strong bonds of fellowship!
- A governmental Church with Apostles, Prophets, Evangelists, Pastors and Teachers functioning out of it!
- A praying and fasting Church!
- A Spirit-Filled and Spirit-Led Church!
- It was at Antioch that they were first called Christians – making them a prototype Church!
- A Resource Centre and a Strong Base of ministry!

- It was from Antioch that Paul and Barnabas went out and came back and reported all that the Lord had done!

It was the place where the prototype of true apostolic ministry was uncovered – Apostles *need* a local home base. In today's Church era, we are seeing some modern day Apostles being deceived by the devil because they feel that they have outgrown the local church and they become a law unto themselves and miss their ultimate purpose in God. That is part of the inaccuracy that we are seeing in some apostolic people.

The Antioch Church was used to settle arguments and problems that arose in other churches and regions. For example the issue of Gentile Christians having to be circumcised by the Jerusalem Church was settled by Paul and Barnabas as they travelled from Antioch to Jerusalem and giving the grace and wisdom that the Lord had given them among the Gentiles and as such they were no longer required to be circumcised.

I like what Apostle John Eckhardt has to say about building Antioch churches, which I refer to as *Fortress churches*:

Characteristics of Apostolic, Territorial Governing Churches
The Antioch church is a model apostolic church. From Antioch the ministries of Barnabas and Paul and later Silas and Paul were released. The Antioch church became a spiritual hub to release apostolic teams that affected nations.

From Antioch God initiated apostolic endeavours that resulted in the planting of strategic churches. The churches of Corinth, Philippi, Colossi, Ephesus and Thessalonica were all formed as a result of the outreach from the church at Antioch.

The church at Antioch represents a governing territorial apostolic church. It represents a church that has a burden for nations and is focused on fulfilling the Great commission.

The characteristic of this church gives it the unique ability to be a strategic church in the plan of God. When a local church has these characteristics, it will impact the regions and territories to which it has been given jurisdiction.

Models are important because they give us a pattern in which to build. We must be careful to build according to Biblical patterns and not the traditions of men. Apostolic churches are prototype churches. They are models that reflect the blueprints and pattern that God is releasing from Heaven. Each generation needs models that will be an impact to that generation. These churches are built by revelation. Apostles are wise builders [1 Corinthians 3:10]. They build according to revelation and are not dependent upon man made patterns that many build by.

Jonathan David states "It takes apostolic wisdom to plant and raise up an apostolic church that resembles Antioch in its nature, structure, ongoing lifestyle and ministry". Most Pastors that I have met think they are building an Antioch type of church. Further conversations however reveal otherwise because most Pastors are building on a blessing model concept rather than on a building model concept.[34]

There are twelve characteristics of the Antioch church I'd like to share. These twelve characteristics when present in a

---

[34] Expounded in Chapter Five of this book!

local church will cause that church to impact its generation. These are constants that we need to have in every generation. Some things change over time but constants remain the same.

1. Breakthrough Believers
"Now those who had been scattered by the persecution that broke out when Stephen was killed travelled as far as Phoenicia, Cyprus and Antioch, spreading the word only among Jews. [20] Some of them, however, men from Cyprus and Cyrene, went to Antioch and began to speak to Greeks also, telling them the good news about the Lord Jesus." [Acts 11:19-20]

Believers who had been scattered from Jerusalem initiated the church at Antioch. When they came to Antioch, they responded to the Holy Spirit's directions and began ministering to the Grecians. Up to this point the Gospel had been preached primarily to the Jews. By preaching to the Grecians, these Believers crossed a cultural barrier and saw great success. Hence the reason we refer to them as *Breakthrough Believers*.

Breakthrough is defined as an act of overcoming or penetrating an obstacle or restriction. It is a major success that permits further progress, as in technology. With each breakthrough provision is made for further progress.

Breakthrough benefits the entire Body of Christ and makes room for advancement. This is the foundation of the church at Antioch. Churches that have Breakthrough Believers will have a foundation to breakthrough and penetrate into various regions. The limitations of culture and religion are broken. These are Believers that respond to the leading of the Holy Spirit without fear. They obey the Holy Spirit even if it means initiating something new. These are pioneer Believers.

Breakthrough Believers are Believers that have broken the limitations of culture, tradition, religion and fear. They have broken the barriers that restrict most people. They are not limited by mindsets that hinder people from launching out and going into unfamiliar territory. They are not bound by the prevailing mentality of the church.

If you desire to build an Antioch church, you must build it with Breakthrough Believers. These are people who have broken out of the normal patterns of religion and tradition. They have overcome the obstacles that prevent most believers from crossing barriers. Breakthrough Believers are the building blocks of the Antioch churches.

Jonathan David gives the following characteristics of Breakthrough Believers based on the Believers who came to Antioch. These breakthrough individuals accomplish the following:

- Pioneer New Moves Of God!
- Able To Move Under Intense Pressure!
- Move Without Compromise!
- Move In Progressive Revelation!
- Move Under Authority!
- Move To Impact Society!

2. Evangelism
As the Believers responded to the Holy Spirit to minister to the Grecians, they broke through into a new evangelistic

endeavour. Their emphasis was on expanding the Kingdom of God through evangelism.

Antioch churches have a foundation of evangelism. The spirit of evangelism is strong in these churches. I call this Breakthrough Evangelism. This is the spiritual ability to penetrate into areas and reach new people groups.

The Great Commission cannot be fulfilled without evangelism. Although the great commission is an apostolic commission, evangelism is an integral part of fulfilling it.

Philip is the New Testament pattern for the Evangelist. He went to Samaria and preached Christ. He cast out demons and healed the sick [Acts 8]. He was able to break open the city of Samaria. He came out of an apostolic community in Jerusalem.

Breakthrough evangelism is a characteristic of Antioch churches. They break the normal barriers and patterns that would limit evangelism. They are able to reach those who have been unreached. Groups of people that were previously overlooked, bypassed, or simply the detached, are touched by breakthrough evangelism.

Antioch churches will see the release of companies of Evangelists. This gift ministry is recognized in Antioch churches. Evangelism is a part of the spiritual DNA of these churches. It is part of their life's blood. They live and grow through evangelism.

Antioch churches gain momentum through breakthrough evangelism. They are open to the Holy Spirit's leading into new areas and people groups. They are not limited to a particular people group. They will not overlook the people groups who are in their own cities. They will develop strategies to reach these people. They will establish a beachhead in every community.

3. Apostolic Input

"Then tidings of these things came unto the ears of the church, which was in Jerusalem; and they sent forth Barnabas, that he should go as far as Antioch." [Acts 11:22]

Antioch churches are those that are willing to receive Apostolic Input. Immediately after the founding of this church, the church at Jerusalem sent Apostle Barnabas. He was an encourager who came to exhort the new church. The sending of Apostle Barnabas by the Jerusalem church represents apostolic input.

Apostolic input strengthens local churches. When churches honour and respect "sent" ones, they will partake of the grace that is upon the "sent" one. Apostolic input helps churches to grow by laying a proper foundation. The church is built upon the foundation of the Apostles and Prophets [Ephesians 2:20.] The new Believers at Antioch began to receive the proper foundation for growth and spiritual development.

New churches need encouragement. Barnabas means son of consolation. He was an encourager who helped strengthen and encouraged new Believers. His maturity was needed for the new work. He was a good man filled with the Holy Ghost and faith.

Churches that lack apostolic input will often remain weak and immature. The church at Antioch began to mature very quickly because of the input of mature ministry gifts. It began to grow both naturally and spiritually. There was a continued spiritual momentum released in this church.

Apostolic input is accomplished by the visit of apostolic and prophetic gifts as well as the visit of apostolic teams. These anointed gifts will strengthen, mature and release Believers into a level of maturity necessary to have impact and influence in regions beyond.

4. Grace
"Who, when he came and had seen the grace of God, was glad and exhorted them all, that with purpose of heart they would cleave unto the Lord." [Acts 11:23]

Antioch churches are churches of grace. Grace is an identifiable mark of these churches. Barnabas noticed the grace that was in this church. Grace is the favour of God. There are blessings that come with this favour. When God's favour is upon a church, it will grow and be a blessing to many.

Churches with grace will flourish and be at the forefront with the demonstration of the Gifts of the Spirit. [1 Corinthians 1:7]. These churches have an abundance of spiritual gifts. This includes the gifts of the Holy Spirit, as well as ministry gifts. Gifted churches have a calling and a commission to bless people. This grace is not given without reason. Grace is God's favour given to be a blessing. Cities, regions and nations can be touched by the grace that is upon a church.

There is a grace to preach, teach and prophesy [gifts of utterance.] There is also grace that brings revelation and insight into the plans and purposes of God. Churches with great grace must not waste this on themselves. They must be stewards of the manifold grace of God. They must disperse and dispense this grace to as many as possible.

The Antioch church became a great blessing to many nations. From Antioch, apostolic grace was released to plant churches and to bless other cities. Rome, Corinth, Ephesus, Philippi and Thessalonica all benefited from the grace that was upon Antioch.

To the extent that grace is on a church is the extent of the blessing it should be to others. Unto whom much is given, much is required. Unto him who has shall more shall be given. These are laws of the Kingdom. God's purposes are fulfilled through grace. Grace gives these churches the ability to do extraordinary things.

There will be an abundance of gifted ministries in Antioch churches. These churches become a spiritual magnet for fivefold ministry gifts. Ministries will also be developed within these churches.

Because there are so many gifts within Antioch churches, there must be a structure to facilitate and release them. One of the ways this is done is through the development and release of teams.

5. Team Ministry
"Then departed Barnabas to Tarsus, for to seek Saul: And when he had found him, he brought him unto Antioch. And it came to pass, that a whole year they assembled themselves with the church, and taught much people, And the disciples were called Christians first in Antioch." [Acts 11:25-26]

After Barnabas came to Antioch and saw the grace that was upon this church, he went to Tarsus to get Saul [Paul]. Barnabas knew the grace that was upon Paul's life and encouraged him to come to Antioch. Barnabas and Saul

[Paul] assembled themselves with the church at Antioch and ministered as a team. Thus they established the team concept at Antioch.

Barnabas and Paul [Saul] would later be released as a team from Antioch. Apostolic ministry is team ministry. A team of Apostles, Prophets and Teachers will have a tremendous impact upon the spiritual condition of a church.

When Jesus came and ministered He gathered together a team around him. He ordained twelve to be with Him. Jesus established the team concept and left us a pattern for breakthrough ministry.

Barnabas and Paul [Saul] laboured as a team to build up the Saints at Antioch. Antioch churches are built through team ministry. They have resident teams and if necessary bring in apostolic teams to build. The church cannot be built by the gift of one single person. We are seeing a shift from the pastoral mode of ministry, where one Shepherd does the majority of ministry to an apostolic mode of ministry where a team labours together to build the church.

Apostles and Prophets work together to lay foundation. These two gifts form a powerful team that is able to release revelation into a church concerning the plans and purposes of God. [Ephesians 3:5] They are governmental gifts that operate in power and authority. They have the power and authority to root out, tear down, throw down, destroy, build and plant [Jeremiah Chapter 1].

Antioch churches develop teams that can be released to the nations. Apostolic and prophetic teams are matured within the church to be released to impact the regions where they were sent. People in an Antioch church understand the team concept of ministry. They have corporate vision and purpose. They understand that no one person can do it alone. They are not jealous or intimidated by other gifts. There is a spirit of cooperation and unity in the Antioch church. There will be a development of apostolic teams, prophetic teams, evangelistic teams; pastoral teams, teaching teams, prayer teams, praise and worship teams and deliverance teams. These teams give Antioch churches the ability to bless cities, regions and nations. The Antioch church is not a one-man show. It is a group of anointed leaders working together towards a common goal.

6. Teaching

Antioch churches are teaching centres. Barnabas and Saul [Paul] taught together as a team for an entire year at Antioch. Antioch Believers were instructed and taught in the Word of God. Without a strong Word base, churches will not be strong enough to breakthrough. Antioch Believers are people of knowledge. They are not ignorant of the Word of God. The Word of God gives the basis for all we do. The church at Antioch was strengthened through the teaching ministry.

Teachers are respected and received in an Antioch church. The Teacher is also a governmental gift. It is mentioned third in [1 Corinthians 12:28.] There is an authority to instruct and impart knowledge to the Saints. This authority and grace must be respected in the church and the opportunity must be given for the teacher to minister. The teaching ministry was one of the distinctive marks of the Antioch church. They ministered along with the Prophets [Acts 13:1].

Teachers should be a part of the presbytery of an Antioch church. They will minister along with the other governmental gifts of the Apostles and Prophets. They also instruct new Believers, who come into the church. To teach means to instruct, to educate, to enlighten, to ground, to explain, to clarify and to interpret. Instructing new Believers is important because they normally would have many questions when confronted with the truth of the gospel.

Antioch churches will teach foundational principles as well as advanced truths. The teaching will be apostolic. Churches must be built upon apostolic doctrine. The teaching is a result of apostolic and prophetic revelation. The teaching level of Antioch churches is high. Many of the Believers will then have an ability to teach others. There is a duplication of the teaching anointing resulting in a company of Teachers and teaching Believers.

These teaching Antioch Believers are able to mentor and train others. They become pattern Believers who are able to explain the Scriptures and defend the truth. They study to show themselves approved unto God, a workman that need not be ashamed, rightly dividing the word of truth [2 Timothy 2:15]. This is an apostolic injunction. Study is reading, reviewing memorizing, researching and meditating. Antioch churches are places that are conducive to the study of the Word of God.

7. Benevolence [Giving]
"And there stood up one of them Agabus, and signified by the Spirit that there should be a great dearth throughout the world; which came to pass in the days of Claudius Caesar. Then the disciples, every man according to his ability, determined to send relief unto the brethren which dwelt in Judea: Which they did, and sent it to the elders by the hands of Barnabas and Saul" [Acts 11:28-30]

The church at Antioch received prophetic ministry. They

honoured the ministry gift of the Prophet and received the Word delivered by Agabus. He foretold of a coming famine in Judea.

The church at Antioch was a benevolent church. They were a giving church that shared and distributed their resources with the churches of Judea. Apostolic distribution is another characteristic of an Antioch church. There is an apostolic mandate to bless the poor. This is seen in Paul's ministry of receiving offerings for the poor Saints of Jerusalem. Apostolic churches should touch poor nations and minister to the needy.

Due to the fact that Antioch churches are giving churches, there is an apostolic grace to give to other churches. Supernatural offerings are common in these churches. There is a spirit of liberality. There is a great grace that results in great giving [Acts 4:33.] They especially minister unto poorer Believers in other regions and nations.

Benevolence is kindness, goodness, graciousness, compassion and humanitarianism. Antioch churches share their wealth with the poor. Benevolence is also a present, a gift, contribution or donation. To be benevolent means to be unselfish, kind-hearted, generous, charitable, liberal and helping.

God blesses Antioch churches with great resources in order to bless others. Apostles and apostolic churches have a grace to distribute. To distribute means to disperse, spread, scatter and administer. Their supernatural giving will mark these churches.

8. Prophetic Ministry
   "And in those days came prophets from Jerusalem unto Antioch. Now there were in the church that was

in Antioch certain Prophets and Teachers" [Acts 11:27; 13:1]

Antioch churches respect and receive prophetic ministry. The prophetic and teaching anointing were dominant gifts in the Antioch church. There was a group of Prophets and Teachers ministering together in the church at Antioch. Prophetic ministry strengthens and confirms the Believer. It brings revelation and refreshing to the Church.

This unique combination of Prophets and Teachers provided an atmosphere for the release of apostolic teams. They both release the Word of the Lord. When the Word of the Lord is strong in a local church, it will create an atmosphere for the release of the plans and purposes of God. Antioch churches are prophetic, teaching churches. When Prophets and Teachers come together as a team, get ready for an apostolic release.

Prophets should be a part of every local church. We are commanded to let the Prophets speak [1 Corinthians Chapter 14.] Antioch churches will have a company of Prophets and prophetic people. The prophetic word releases life. Prophetic input keeps these churches fresh and on the cutting edge of what God is doing. The prophetic ministry is strong in these churches because Prophets are honoured and received. People are changed when they come into contact with a company of Prophets. As Prophets prophesy and minister the Spirit of God is released over the lives of those who are ministered to. People are lifted to new levels. The prophetic word activates and initiates people into their destinies. The word is creative and releases the plans and purposes of God.

Prophets along with Apostles bring revelation to the Church [Ephesians 3:5]. They also lay a foundation [Ephesians

2:20]. Antioch churches will have Believers strong in revelation and foundation. They will have insight into the plans and purposes of God as a result of prophetic ministry.

9. Plurality of Leadership [Presbytery]
"Now there were in the church that was at Antioch certain prophets and teachers; as Barnabas, and Simeon that was called Niger, and Lucius of Cyrene, and Manean which had been brought up with Herod the tetrarch, and Saul." [Acts 13:1]

Notice the leadership combination at Antioch. The team at Antioch was unique. They had professionals, dignitaries and strong ministry gifts in their leadership teams. Barnabas had been a Levitical priest whereas Saul [Paul] was highly educated in the ways of Judaism. Manaen was brought up in the courts of Herod the Tetrarch. Simeon was called Niger, which means black. Antioch represents a church that does not discriminate based on colour or background. The leadership in Antioch represents a multicultural mix that represents the Kingdom of God.

The anointing upon a Believer's life is received in an Antioch church. Their gift is respected. They are challenged to fulfil their destinies and are taught to overcome their cultural barriers. They are not judged in the natural, but discerned in the spirit. People are not held back by the insecurities and prejudices of leadership. Cultural bias had been broken by a spirit of love and unity.

Apostolic churches receive people based upon their gifting and character, rather than upon race or culture. The spirit of racism and discrimination is broken in an Antioch church. People are attracted to these churches because of the anointing and the apostolic spirit that is within them. These churches will attract people of all backgrounds because they are Kingdom churches. They manifest the Kingdom of God, which is above our particular culture and people group.

Antioch churches will be places where people can receive training and be released as leaders. Leaders are developed in an Antioch church. They are raised up quickly. As Barnabas and Paul ministered in Antioch we see a group of leaders being raised up quickly. People are challenged to rise up quickly, they are challenged to rise up and embrace their calling. They are expected to fulfil these callings and obey the Lord. All gifts are recognized in these churches. They have a revelation of the importance of all the gifts and ministries.

There is a plurality of leadership in Antioch churches. Plurality is what gives these churches strength. They are not limited to one or a few gifts. They understand the blessing of diversity and abundance. A team of Prophets and Teachers at Antioch birthed a strong apostolic move. This is the key to birthing and releasing strong apostolic moves throughout the Earth.

10. Ministering to the Lord
    "As they ministered to the lord and fasted." [Acts 13:2]

Ministry to the Lord characterizes the Antioch church. There is a spirit of worship in these churches. Worship releases the spirit of prophecy [Revelation 19:10]. It provides an atmosphere to hear the Voice of God. As they fasted they developed sensitivity to the Holy Spirit. Fasting is the Biblical way of humbling oneself [Psalms Chapter 35.] As we humble ourselves we receive grace.

Although this was a church of grace, they continued to receive more grace through fasting and ministering to the

Lord. Apostolic grace was released. This was a sending grace. They were able to hear the voice of God and release two of their most notable ministers for apostolic ministry.

Fasting and prayer has always been a way to minister to the Lord. Anna ministered to the Lord in this way for many years [Luke 2:36-38.] Her ministry contributed with bringing in the Messiah. She was a part of birthing deliverance for Israel and the world. Churches that minister to the Lord in fasting and prayer will be a part of birthing new ministries. As Prophets and Teachers ministered to the Lord and fasted the apostolic ministry of Barnabas and Paul were released.

Ministering to the Lord is important in Antioch churches. To minister means to wait upon. They that wait upon the Lord shall renew their strength. Antioch Believers wait upon the Lord for direction. Their obedience comes out of hearing the Voice of the Lord. They are sensitive to God's Voice. They cherish the Voice of the Lord and realize the importance of ministering to the Lord.

11. Prayer and Fasting
    "And when they had fasted and prayed, and laid their hands on them, they sent them away." [Acts 13:3]

Prayer is the power source of the apostolic. Prayer releases the apostolic anointing. Prayer causes God to "send forth" labourers into the harvest. The Apostles gave themselves to prayer and the ministry of the Word [Acts 13:3.] Antioch churches pray without ceasing [1Thessolians 5:17. They are strong in corporate prayer [Acts 4:31.] They labour in prayer [Colossians 4:12.] They pray with the spirit and with the understanding [1 Corinthians 14:15.]

Fasting is also part of apostolic ministry [2 Corinthians 11:27.]

Fasting is an act of humility. It is a declaration in the spirit that we are entirely dependent upon God. Sent ones are dependent upon the sender. Their power and authority come from the sender.

Antioch churches are houses of prayer. They are strong bases of prayer and intercession. Prayer and fasting are supernatural weapons that destroy strongholds of darkness. Leadership is released through prayer and fasting. Elders are ordained through prayer and fasting. Great power and anointing is released through prayer and fasting.

The level of power and anointing is high in an Antioch church because of prayer and fasting. The leadership is committed to prayer and fasting. The result will be signs, wonders, and miracles on a consistent basis. Prayer and fasting is a way to establish beachheads and break open difficult territories, in order to advance the Kingdom of God in those places. It is a platform in which strong ministries are built. Fasting gives Antioch churches the ability to build the old waste places. They establish the foundations of many generations. They become the repairers of the breach and the restorer of paths to dwell in [Isaiah 58:6, 12.]

12. Sending Church [Releasing]
    "And when they had fasted and prayed, and laid their hands on them, they sent them away." [Acts 13:3]

The Prophets and Teachers at Antioch responded to the Holy Spirit and send out an apostolic team consisting of Barnabas and Saul [Paul]. The Antioch church is a sending church. Apostolic people and churches revolve around the concept of sending and being sent.

Antioch became an apostolic mission base for developing and

releasing apostolic teams. The Biblical pattern of planting and building churches is through apostolic teams. These teams give the local church the ability to reach out beyond their region into other regions and nations. Churches are then able to impact other regions and territories.

Antioch was a key to the establishing of the strategic churches of Corinth, Ephesus, Thessalonica and Philippi. These strategic churches in turn became governing churches that affected other regions and territories. A church success should not be measured by how many Saints/Believers come in but also by how many are released and sent out. Antioch has a "sending" mentality and understanding of the fulfilling of the Great Commission requires sending.

God the Father sends. Jesus sends. The Holy Spirit sends. The church sends. Sending is part of the strategy of the Godhead, and it should also be a part of the strategy of the church. The apostolic spirit is a sending spirit. Antioch churches will develop a strategy for developing and releasing apostolic teams. With a "sending" mentality as a principle in an Antioch church, they are quick to hear the Voice of God and to release those whom God says to release. They become sending stations that release the anointing of God throughout the Earth.

Churches are planted and nations are affected. One of the greatest joys is to become a "sender." God the Father, Son and Holy Spirit are all "senders." This is the very nature of the Godhead. Antioch churches will have this nature. They are partakers of the divine nature. They operate with the mentality of the Godhead. Antioch churches know the importance of "sending." They have a strategy that incorporates "sending." They are able to extend their borders by releasing teams to the nations. The teams "sent" out operate in the authority of the "sending" church. They are backed by the prayers and finances of the local church. Without "sending" the Church will not be able to fulfil the great Commission.

Antioch churches are churches of impact because they are "sending" churches. They "send" out ministries in obedience to the Voice and direction of the Holy Spirit. Their success is dependent upon obeying the Lord in "sending." They do not hold back from releasing and "sending" those whom God has released to be "sent." They operate in the cycle of training and releasing. When leaders are trained and released, new ones are raised up to replace them. There is a continual reproduction, which is a Kingdom principle.

This is the precise pattern God intends for the local church today. Through training, teaching, discipleship and relationship, God begins to empower by the Holy Spirit individuals in preparation for greater service. This is the natural progression of spiritual things. God sends someone out to allow someone else to step into a place of service and leadership. The church in Antioch was a dynamic, powerful church. God's grace abounded. This is most clearly presented in the 13th Chapter of the Book of Acts. In this Chapter, Barnabas, Saul [Paul] and the church take another step in their journey, building the type of church God really desires. In the church at Antioch, a revised model for the expansion of the Kingdom of God is found.

In essence Antioch was a *Fortress Church*! Antioch was a *Divine Stronghold*! Oh yes do you think it was the devil that originally established strongholds? No he is a copycat and a weak one at that. Our God is *A Fortress* to His Church. Jesus Christ The Builder is building us as A *Fortress Church*!

> "Great is the LORD, and most worthy of praise, in the city of our God, his holy mountain. 2 Beautiful in its

loftiness, the joy of the whole earth, like the heights of Zaphon is Mount Zion, the city of the Great King. 3 *God is in her citadels; he has shown himself to be her fortress.*" Psalms 48:1-3 [Italics Added]

☞ CHAPTER 5

FROM BLESSING MODEL TO BUILDING MODEL

Apostolic Vision Of The New Testament Church! The church that will thrive in the 21st century will not be anchored in stale forms and programs, but will forge boldly into new territories, possessing them in the Name of the King, it will the church with the building mentality. It will be a *"Fortress Church!"*

One of the characteristics of this "new kind of church" is a people who will embrace the Scriptural *building model* rather than just the *blessing model*.

Jesus said in Matthew 16:18 "I will be build my church"!
The question we have to ask ourselves is how is He doing this? We know that He is using Apostles and Prophets, along with Evangelists, Pastors and Teachers to accomplish this task, as revealed in the Letter to the church at Ephesus by Apostle Paul [Ephesians 4:11-16.]

So in essence Jesus is building the "hardware" of the Church [we do not determine which person get saved and is added to the Church; Jesus does that]. Apostles are mandated and ordained to build the "software" of the Church; that is the internal dynamics.

In order to fully understand the New Testament building process as revealed in 1 Peter 2:1-12 – Let's read verses 5-10

"Coming to Him as to a living stone, rejected indeed by

men, but chosen by God *and* precious, ⁵ *you also, as living stones, are being built up a spiritual house, a holy priesthood, to offer up spiritual sacrifices acceptable to God through Jesus Christ.* ⁶ Therefore it is also contained in the Scripture," *Behold, I lay in Zion A chief cornerstone, elect, precious, And he who believes on Him will by no means be put to shame."* ⁷ Therefore, to you who believe, *He is* precious; but to those who are disobedient, *"The stone which the builders rejected Has become the chief cornerstone,"* ⁸ and *"A stone of stumbling And a rock of offense."* They stumble, being disobedient to the word, to which they also were appointed. ⁹ But you *are* a chosen generation, a royal priesthood, a holy nation, His own special people, that you may proclaim the praises of Him who called you out of darkness into His marvellous light; ¹⁰ who once *were* not a people but *are* now the people of God, who had not obtained mercy but now have obtained mercy." [Italics Added]

So we understand that the Born-Again Believer is the Stone that the Lord is using to build His Church... However, in order for us to fully understand this Building Process it is necessary for us to revisit the original Temple that was built to House the Presence of God.

The Prototype is what is known as Solomon's Temple and can be found in 1 Kings Chapters 5 to 8! While we would not be reading all those verses I would like to visit a few of them, which show a careful, well-documented plan for its construction!

Let us briefly visit 1 Kings 6:2-10
"The temple that King Solomon built for the LORD was sixty cubits long, twenty wide and thirty high. 3 The portico at the front of the main hall of the temple

extended the width of the temple, that is twenty cubits, and projected ten cubits from the front of the temple. 4 He made narrow windows high up in the temple walls. 5 Against the walls of the main hall and inner sanctuary he built a structure around the building, in which there were side rooms. 6 The lowest floor was five cubits wide, the middle floor six cubits and the third floor seven. He made offset ledges around the outside of the temple so that nothing would be inserted into the temple walls. 7 *In building the temple, only blocks dressed at the quarry were used, and no hammer, chisel or any other iron tool was heard at the temple site while it was being built.* 8 The entrance to the lowest floor was on the south side of the temple; a stairway led up to the middle level and from there to the third. 9 So he built the temple and completed it, roofing it with beams and cedar planks. 10 And he built the side rooms all along the temple. The height of each was five cubits, and they were attached to the temple by beams of cedar." [Italics Added]

Verse 7: The original temple was built with "*stone*" and *not* bricks. Today, "*stone*" represents the Born-Again, Spirit-Filled, Believer, who is also known as a *living stone*. Just as a stone is known in the natural state, similarly a "*living stone*" [Believer] can also be compared today as we build the Church. Stones are not all the same and they are not man-made, they are different in shape, size, colour and texture. Unlike bricks which are man-made and all are the same, shape, size, colour and texture.

The religious systems of men build with bricks! Building with bricks is a principle in the world's system as revealed by the Egyptians. They gave the children of Israel bricks to build with in Egypt [Exodus 1:11-14] but the Church of Jesus Christ is built with stone, *living stones*!

Stone That Was Finished In The Quarry:
We read that the stones that were used in building Solomon's Temple [the Prototype], were chipped or prepared in the Quarry, away from the building site, I believe it is the same with the *living stones* that are being used in building The Church of Jesus Christ!

Stone finished in the Quarry – This finished dimension is away from the peering eye. Therefore life circumstances or whatever God decides to use to shape us is done in order for us to be fit for the Master's use. This speaks also of character that has been developed and shaped. It is like the iceberg where all one sees is one tenth of its size above the water with the other nine tenths under the water and unseen. Similarly, we the *living stones* that are being used by God should reflect that which is hidden and must be greater than that which is seen. The foundation of our lives must be strong and pure!

As the Apostle Peter was about to bring the revelation concerning us the Born-Again, Spirit-Filled, Believers as the *living stones* being used by the Lord to build His Church, this is what he shared:

1 Peter 3:1-3
> "Wherefore laying aside all malice, and all guile, and hypocrisies, and envies, and all evil speakings, ²As newborn babes, desire the *sincere milk of the word, that ye may grow thereby*: ³If so be ye have tasted that the Lord is gracious." [KJV Italics Added]

Here Apostle Peter is establishing the well-known fact that *character* is of the utmost importance in the heart of God.

The stones that He will ultimately use will be those whose characters are well built. Character or integrity ensures that the stone is solid, sure and steadfast. In essence it is *"sincere!"* Sincere comes from two Latin words "sine and cere" and means *"without wax."* The etymology of this word sincere is very interesting. Let me briefly share it with you:

Prior to the 15th Century the world went through what we have come to know as the Dark Ages [a period of time when there was no new inventions or revelation]. Coming out of that dark period we saw the emergence of the era known as the Renaissance and the birth of new and wonderful things happening across the earth. It was during this time we saw the emergence of the Wittenberg printing press which greatly benefited the sum total of the population on the globe. Also around that time there were many gifted Artisans rising up and great sculptures were hewn out of solid chunks of stone and marble. These products would fetch great prices from the affluent members of society and as such their work became a very lucrative business. However, there also arose some counterfeit "quacks" or Artisans lacking any shred of integrity! – Rather than beginning again, they sculpted and produced items of inferior quality, which was not apparent to the naked eye. Their wares looked good, but they practiced unscrupulous acts by sealing up the cracks or fissures in their sculptures with molten wax. As such, they would dupe the unsuspecting art aficionado. After the purchase was made and some time would pass, the unsuspecting buyer would be the victim of fraudulent tactics, as the heat would eventually melt the wax and reveal the treasure for the piece of inferior junk that it was.

It was the backdrop of this scenario that they developed a terminology called *"sine cere"* the Latin for *"without wax."* This is where we get our English word sincere. The prospective buyer would ask the sculptor—is your sculptor *"sine cere."* The point to be derived from this is: The emerging Apostles along with the other Five-Fold ministry gifts who are to equip the Saints must work in sincerity otherwise when the heat of life's circumstances and ministry bear down upon the Saints without being grounded in sincerity, the pressure would quickly reveal character flaws!

Hence the reason we need people that are "sine cere" in the *Fortress Church* so that we can build correctly. We do not want when the battle heats up that people begin to melt, because their lives are filled of wax. Hence there must be a love for the "sine cere" Word of God that will shape us. There are NO cracks in the Word of God. His Word is infallible and is able to build us up! Able to sanctify us and make us clean and holy! It is His Word that we are to hide in our hearts so that we would not sin against the Lord!

Here Are Some Of The Examples Of The Usage Of This Word—Sincere:

1 Corinthians 5:6-8
> "Your glorying *is* not good. Do you not know that a little leaven leavens the whole lump? 7 Therefore purge out the old leaven, that you may be a new lump, since you truly are unleavened. For indeed Christ, our Passover, was sacrificed for us. 8 Therefore let us keep the feast, not with old leaven, nor with the leaven of malice and wickedness, but with the unleavened *bread* of sincerity and truth."

2 Corinthians 1:8-12
> "For we do not want you to be ignorant, brethren, of our trouble which came to us in Asia: that we were burdened beyond measure, above strength, so that we despaired even of life. 9 Yes, we had the sentence

of death in ourselves that we should not trust in ourselves but in God who raises the dead, 10 who delivered us from so great a death, and does deliver us; in whom we trust that He will still deliver *us,* 11 you also helping together in prayer for us, that thanks may be given by many persons on our behalf for the gift *granted* to us through many.12 For our boasting is this: the testimony of our conscience that we conducted ourselves in the world in simplicity and godly sincerity, not with fleshly wisdom but by the grace of God, and more abundantly toward you."

2 Corinthians 2:12-17

"Furthermore, when I came to Troas to *preach* Christ's gospel, and a door was opened to me by the Lord, 13 I had no rest in my spirit, because I did not find Titus my brother; but taking my leave of them, I departed for Macedonia. 14 Now thanks *be* to God who always leads us in triumph in Christ, and through us diffuses the fragrance of His knowledge in every place. 15 For we are to God the fragrance of Christ among those who are being saved and among those who are perishing. 16 To the one *we are* the aroma of death *leading* to death, and to the other the aroma of life *leading* to life. And who *is* sufficient for these things? 17 For we are not, as so many, peddling the word of God; but as of sincerity, but as from God, we speak in the sight of God in Christ."

Titus 2:1-10

"But speak thou the things which become sound doctrine: 2That the aged men be sober, grave, temperate, sound in faith, in charity, in patience. 3The aged women likewise, that they be in behaviour as becometh holiness, not false accusers, not given to much wine, teachers of good things; 4That they may teach the young women to be sober, to love their husbands, to love their children, 5To be discreet, chaste, keepers at home, good, obedient to their own husbands, that the word of God be not blasphemed. 6Young men likewise exhort to be sober minded. 7In all things shewing thyself a pattern of good works: in doctrine shewing uncorruptness, gravity, sincerity, 8Sound speech, that cannot be condemned; that he that is of the contrary part may be ashamed, having no evil thing to say of you. 9Exhort servants to be obedient unto their own masters, and to please them well in all things; not answering again; 10Not purloining, but shewing all good fidelity; that they may adorn the doctrine of God our Saviour in all things." [KJV]

Let Us Be "Sine Cere" – Without Wax!

So That No Hammer Or Chisel Or Any Iron Tool Was Heard In The Temple While It Was Being Built: I submit to you that the noise from spiritual tools making adjustment on living stones – represents schisms, dissentions and discord among the Saints. It also represents the effort to be used in trying to place individual stones in the wrong position as there must be no forcing the fit. The joining must be right or there will be dissonance in the ear of the Spirit that will result in a cessation of the building process. It is an ugly sight to behold when someone who is not called to a particular office or position in the Body of Christ trying to function/fit in that position or office. That is why so many today are setting themselves up to be called "false prophet" and "false apostle" and "false minister," because they are self appointed and are out of order and placement!

Stones With Cracks Cannot Take Heavy Burdens; They Will Eventually Crack Up Causing A Weak Point In The Building:

In the *Fortress Church* leadership is taken very seriously. Part of the problem that we are experiencing today is with several so called "high profile" leaders falling into sin and then refusing to step down or take any form of serious corrective measures/counsel, but instead they continue as if nothing ever went wrong! This is why it is not wise to set people into leadership positions prematurely, because they will eventually crack and then most ministries paste wax in the crack [cover the sin or fault] and after awhile that ministry is destroyed. The Bible admonishes us to confess our faults, if we have any! [James 5:16]

> "*Confess your faults* one to another, and pray one for another, that ye may be healed. The effectual fervent prayer of a righteous man availeth much." [KJV Italics Added]

A fault is a defect in your foundation or character, confess it, get help and move on!

As a Born-Again Believer in Jesus Christ we must understand/remember that we have been given a brand new citizenship. Although we live and function on earth we are Citizens of Heaven and as such we must operate by Heaven's standards.

Ephesians 2:19 declare, that our passports are from Heaven. This is not some theory but rather, a stated fact, that we are Citizens from Heaven!

Not only are we Sons of God, but we are also Citizens of Heaven. Please understand that Heaven is a real physical place. It is not some ethereal place out there; it is as *real* as it gets. It can support and sustain human life forms! Let's just establish this fact before proceeding, as we have empirical evidence that real people went to Heaven!

- [35]Enoch was the first recorded human being to physically and literally go to Heaven.
- [36]Elijah was the second – he went up in a tempest. Have you ever read the Book of Ezekiel? – There are some Chapters describing things in Heaven that nobody could accurately preach on. Heaven is a real place and has an ordered society. Elijah wrote about a wheel within wheels with eyes and sound. It is indescribable to a degree, but certainly it is not referring to UFOs.
- Jesus went up to Heaven in a Body. He went through great pains to prove that He was made of matter. Thomas doubted until he was able to put his fingers through Jesus' flesh. Jesus proved it and said to him therefore spirits do not have flesh. – Luke 24: 36-45, John 20:24-28

We are Citizens of Heaven and we need to focus on this and understand it fully. We are truly *"aliens" from another planet* and as such we need to know our *Identity* and function while on this planet called Earth. Philippians 3:20 states:

> "For our citizenship is in heaven, from which we also eagerly wait for the Saviour, the Lord Jesus Christ..."

In his letter to the Philippians the Apostle Paul was declaring to them that just as Jesus was from Heaven, even so our citizenship is in Heaven. This was a very powerful truth at that time and to that group of Believers and it also

---

[35] Genesis 5:24   Hebrews 11:5
[36] 2 Kings 2:11

reveals a powerful truth to us even today!

Now let me share a bit with you about Philippi and why it is the Apostle Paul could share this truth there; that was so powerful and liberating.

The Church in Philippi was situated in a very unusual place. Philippi was a city in Macedonia – what is known as modern Greece. Philippi was named after Phillip the 2nd, the father of Alexander the Great. Phillip was the architect of the Grecian empire and the fulfilment of Daniel's prophecy two hundred years before he was born. This city was birthed in 350 BC and it was a centre for Greek culture with its temples, a library and a debating forum.

In 42 BC a fellow named Mark Anthony and another Augustus Octavia [who later became Augustus Caesar] went and attacked the armies of Brutus and Cassius [these were the guys who had killed Julius Caesar.] After they killed Julius Caesar the armies of Brutus and Cassius fled to Greece and it was there that they were annihilated. In honour of this victory the Roman Government conferred the honour of becoming a part of Rome upon Philippi. Instantly everyone living in Philippi automatically became Roman citizens. They had full rights and privileges just as someone living back in Rome, Italy.

Now, you can understand why the Apostle Paul was using Philippi to convey his message – they had a natural situation that brought a certain level of thought and understanding that he used to express a valuable spiritual truth! In the same way that Philippi was in Greece about 1300 km [900 miles] away from Rome over the Adriatic Sea, and that its citizens were under Roman jurisdiction as though they lived in Rome, the Philippians fully understood what Apostle Paul was speaking about. They were Roman citizens in a sea of Grecian influence and they functioned like Romans. So Paul was saying to them – the same way you now live like Romans in Greece, live like Citizens of Heaven upon the earth!

As seen in Philippians 2:15, they understood this lifestyle of living contrary to one's surrounding influences! He was saying to them that in the same way you now live as Romans in a Grecian culture, in like manner you could shine as lights and live Kingdom in the midst of a perverse and crooked culture!

What is the application for us? We live upon the earth but our standards, rules, laws, that govern our behaviour and actions come from another place – Heaven! We do not have to separate ourselves from the world to live under Heaven's standard; we must do it just like the Philippians, veritable Roman citizens in Greece! Every time God places an Identity in us it represents *upward motion* and once we move away from that place it is always described as a *fall, downwards*! We are Citizens of Heaven – upwards, not downwards on earth!

This is exactly what happened to the first Adam; let's take a journey back to the first man Adam and see what happened to him.

In Genesis 1:26-28 We Read The Following:
"Then God said, "Let Us *make man in Our image*, according to Our likeness; *let them have dominion* over the fish of the sea, over the birds of the air, and over the cattle, over all the earth and over every creeping thing that creeps on the earth." 27 So God created man in His own image; in the image of God He created him; male and female He created them. 28 Then *God blessed them*, and God said to them, "*Be fruitful and multiply*; fill the earth and subdue it; have

dominion over the fish of the sea, over the birds of the air, and over every living thing that moves on the earth." [Italics Added]

Man was initially created in the image and likeness of God; that word "image" comes from a root word in Hebrew meaning a shadow or a phantom. It is as if God passed by a wall, His Shadow was cast and He said let us make man like this. This happened before man fell and corrupted that image.

As a result an internal reformation needs to take place as the effects of the first Adam's fall still affect many of us today. Many Believers even though they are saved by the Precious Blood of Jesus, are still suffering the effects of the fall at one level or another. Now there are three things that I want to identify in this original plan of God for mankind, *both* male and female:

- The power of dominion!
- They were blessed by God!
- They had the power of productivity and multiplication!

However, mankind lost a significant amount of what was initially given to them because of disobedience to God and their subsequent fall. In an attempt to fully understand what was lost by the fall we need to revisit the very inception of creation and view several things, which occurred at that time; for example:

In Genesis 2:24-25; we see the power of vision that Almighty God possessed; even though there were no children or any concept of having children; the Lord introduced the concept of a man leaving his mother and father and cleaving unto his wife. This to me is very interesting; there were no children as yet at that time, so the concept of "father and mother" did not yet exist; however, God had already set up the parameters as though this already occurred! He sets up the idea of a bond between a man and his wife that is much stronger than paternal bonding! We were designed to leave and cleave to our mates for life!

Before the fall, they were naked and not ashamed – they had no concept of nakedness as they were Heavenly-minded. They had no point of reference for nakedness, until sin entered and they *fell*! They fell from that Heavenly realm and they lost something – they lost their true Identity:

It is recorded in Genesis 3:6-7 that the moment they sinned [disobeyed God] "their eyes were open" – it was not that they could not see before, but the reality of their perceptions changed and they were now controlled by a different realm – the earth realm! At that very moment their thought life got rewired. Adam saw the physical features of his wife and she his, and something happened that relegated their life to mere humans.

Do you realize that Adam never perspired before the fall; did not think about his private parts, had no concept of hard work. They did not realize that they were naked, but as soon as they fell they were relegated to the flesh and they began looking at their nakedness and a new realm was introduced in their hearts to now define themselves; how each other looked; a new level of sexuality entered the human race and this has worsened as time elapsed. Even to this day for most of mankind beauty is skin deep! But that is not how it should be for us the Born-Again Believer, the ones who have and are experiencing *"internal change"*. The Flesh must not define us; we are not *naked* – we are to be clothed in Him – in

Christ! God then asked them; "who told you, you were naked?" God knew that they had entered the earth realm and that their perceptions were changed – He declared to them: "you have eaten of the tree I commanded you not to".

Genesis 3:8 records that in their sinful state they heard the Voice of God! That to me is very interesting, and here is why. When man sinned the serpent tempted them in the realm of sight; as is recorded in Genesis 3:6-7 and he is still doing that to this very day. However, that is not the point I want you to see here; this is it – Even in the fall God was very merciful and prepares a way for mankind to be restored. In order for mankind to be Born-Again or for us to be restored to the state prior to Adam and Eve's fall; God uses our ability to hear to introduce Himself to us. Do you see this? As God is restoring us what does He do? – He moves us away from the sight realm and shifts us into the hearing realm – *"Faith comes by hearing and hearing the Word of God! Today if you hear My voice do not harden your heart."* – That to be is simply put, Awesome!

Another piece of evidence that mankind lost something when they fell is recorded Genesis 3:16. Here we read that childbearing entered and that it would be accompanied with pain. The fact that God was now declaring this revealed that it was never in His original plan. Also that verse goes on to tell us that the male of the species was going to have rule over the female; another point proving that this was not God's original intent. The woman's desire was now turned towards her husband and he was going to dominate her – all which was part of the curse. This was never to be so; Adam and Eve were to walk as equals. There is now a war of the sexes, women want to be men and men want to rule over women; that was never ever God's intention.

Another cursed was heaped upon mankind because of the

fall and it is recorded in Genesis 3:17-19. The ground from which mankind was formed was cursed and Adam had to work a cursed land [instead of a blessed land] and now had to sweat to in order to have food to eat. He became subject to the hostility of his environment!

Then we read of the final curse, which I think was the most hurtful of all the curses heaped upon mankind; and that was the fact that they were going to return back to the dust from which they came. From the fall of mankind life has been progressively getting worse as the reality of the curse is taking effect. I tell you it is a sad thing to be born in sin, live a fallen lifestyle and then die and end back up in the dust without any hope. But thank God, He has provided a way for us to be eternally changed and enter into what the first Adam should have walked in. So in the midst of this digression into shame and death, in steps the second man, the last Adam, Jesus Christ; born in the earth, born of a woman and begin to manifest the true qualities of a Citizen of Heaven living upon the earth. He conquers death and sets us free from the effects and the curse of the first man's fall, providing the way for us to live a victorious live, just as He did!

Are you seeing this – Jesus lived a complete victorious life – He was truly what I would like to call the Pattern Son. Then God draws Him out of the earth back into Heaven and begins to call us towards His lifestyle as the Pattern! So in the midst of every thing that we see in the earth it is designed to call us *downward* to death and dust. However, there is a summons or a call from Heaven that is constantly calling us *upward in Christ*! Hear me, the whole divine plan in life is for fallen man to answer that Call and begin to progressively walk upward to that *High Call*. He wants us to step into our true identity as Born-Again Believers, an identity that is not rooted in the earth realm, but one that proclaims and identifies us as Citizens of Heaven.

Again the Apostle Paul in his letter to Saints at Philippi does a superb job in explaining this awesome reality as he writes – declaring to them that even though you are living on the earth, your citizenship is in Heaven. He realized this concept/revelation out of his own experiences. He was writing out of the conviction and understanding that the God of Heaven laid on him an upward call or prize so he was defining his life by a totally different standard. He was describing his whole life's mission from the perspective of an understanding that there was an upward call upon him and he had to manifest this upward call while still living upon the earth. He succinctly describes in the following passage of Scripture.

> "Not that I have already *attained*, or am already perfected; but I press on, *that I may lay hold of that for which Christ Jesus has also laid hold of me.* 13 Brethren, I do not count myself to have apprehended; but one thing I do, forgetting those things which are behind and reaching forward to those things which are ahead, 14 I press toward the goal for the prize of *the upward call of God in Christ Jesus*. Therefore *let us, as many as are mature*, have this mind; and if in anything you think otherwise, God will reveal even this to you. 16 Nevertheless, to the degree that we have already *attained*, let us walk by the same rule, let us be of the same mind." [Philippians 3:12-16 Italics Added]

> "Not that I have already *obtained* all this, or have already been made perfect, but I press on *to take hold of that for which Christ Jesus took hold of me.*

Brothers, I do not consider myself yet to have taken hold of it. But one thing I do: Forgetting what is behind and straining toward what is ahead, I press on toward the goal to win the prize for which God has *called me heavenward in Christ Jesus*. All of *us who are mature* should take such a view of things. And if on some point you think differently, that too God will make clear to you. 16 Only let us live up to what we have already *attained*." [NIV Italics Added]

Attainment and maturity speak of a process. What the Apostle Paul was speaking about was not referring to the life to come but rather about our current life here and now on planet earth! God was calling him upward or heavenward; however, most times when we read this we think about the final reality. We are always defining the end process, waiting to be caught up to meet Him! But this is not what Apostle Paul is speaking about, he is dealing with the *now* reality – God is calling us Heavenward to a higher lifestyle; to live here on the planet called earth as Citizens of Heaven! In essence Apostle Paul was living with a clear understanding and perspective that he had to manifest a heavenly lifestyle while walking on planet earth. That is why he described himself as being in a constant upward, forward, press towards maturity. He was declaring that his life was not caught up in an earthly press, even though he was living on earth; no, instead he was caught up heavenward and as such we also need to be focused. And in order for us to press upward and heavenward there has to be an internal change in us.

However, the fact that the Apostle Paul was sharing this with the Saints at Philippi is very significant. Now understand something here that is vital to our pressing onwards and upwards. When Mark Anthony and Julius Octavia declared the former citizens of Greece to be Roman citizens, they were indeed Roman Citizens! However, they had to now learn the laws, culture and lifestyle of Rome. I am sure it took them a number of years to acquire all the knowledge needed to fully be a Roman citizen, so when Paul began explaining this new concept to them, they fully understood what he was talking about!

Another point to remember is this; everything that we are in this life, we have learned. For example what makes a Chinese person a Chinese? Is it their language or the colour of their skin or the construct of their eyes? If a Caucasian Canadian goes off to China to live for a few decades, that person will be speaking the Chinese language and flowing in some of the customs of that society.

They will identify themselves as Chinese more readily as that of being Canadian. This would be so because we become what we learn. In like manner we have to learn the language and culture of the Kingdom of Heaven. We have to become unlearned in the value system of the earth and the flesh and learn to walk in Kingdom Lifestyle! The same way we learned the lessons that constructed our personality from the time that we were born, we too can unlearn the very same things and be shaped and formed by the things of the Kingdom. We can be transformed in the spirit of our mind and become our true identity – An *"Operational Son"* of God!

This is exactly what has been happening to us from the day we got saved – The Lord has been reconstructing us and causing us to become un-learned from the former value system of the world. He is doing an internal work in us by His Spirit and as such He is re-structuring and teaching us the value and lifestyle of His Kingdom!

In Ephesians 1:3 it states that He has blessed us with every spiritual blessing in the Heavenly places in Christ – We cannot access this living from an earthly or earth-bound mentality or lifestyle in the flesh! The blessing is in the Heavenlies!

It further states in Ephesians 1:20-23 that He gave us Dominion over every name [human condition!] Even death has no power over us because of the finished work of Christ. When we die, we are instantly with the Lord. This is so powerful! Death is the final enemy that tries to keep us down!

As one continues reading the Book of Ephesians there is something very powerful and important in the process and progression of the Scripture. We see that Jesus Christ [The Anointed One] was attacked by the final enemy, death – but God raised Him from the dead! Then God caused Him to rise *far above every*:

- Principality
- Authority
- Power
- Dominion
- Every name in this world [whether it is Buddha, Allah, Hare-Krishna, Si-Baba, President X or Y, Prime Minister X or Y, Your name, you name it, He is *above*!] Also every name in the world to come...

He has put *all things* under His Feet and then made Him to be the Head over the Church. He has ascended into Heaven and has taken His place on the Right Hand of God. Every time the Name of Jesus Christ is mentioned it is associated with an "up" position in Heaven. Our destination is that same location. Once we understand this we cannot be cast down or depressed for very long, as we must bounce back, if the revelation of this truth is in us! According to Ephesians 2:1-7, we have been *raised up* [remember, we have not left the earth; so he is talking about lifestyle] to a higher level because of salvation. As such we do not have to be influenced by the earth realm's low-level thinking anymore. I am not talking about low-level thinking in terms of academics or lack thereof; I am referring to fleshly or carnal thinking/lifestyle, etc. We can begin to express our true identity even though we currently live in a hostile environment.

The writer of the letter to the Ephesians continues to make some very salient and pertinent points, which I would like to briefly highlight. In Ephesians 2:5-6 it is made absolutely clear that while we were still dead in sins [please note that there isn't one person alive today that was around when this happened; but we are all include,] He made us *Alive In Christ* – So *In Christ* is the only way that we can be made to truly live. The writer continues by revealing to us that just as Jesus Christ was raised from the dead [death being our final enemy]; the Born-Again Believer was also raised together *In Christ*! Not only that but we have been made to sit *together with Christ in the Heavenlies*. This is not just some theoretical statement; it is a fact, just as true, as when the citizens of Philippi became Roman citizens when Mark Anthony and Augustus Octavia [Julius Caesar] invaded Greece and took their Grecian city and made it a colony of Rome.

All these things point to the reason why we hear and respond to a Heavenly Call! Everything hinges on the reality that Christ has done all these things!

Verse 7 goes on to speak of where God wants to get us to – we have not seen the extent of what God has in store. We first have to cultivate a new level of lifestyle based on the reality of what Jesus did and then we can step into the reality of our calling! I am telling you Saints; once you begin to think like this, all kinds of self-esteem problems will be fixed in your life. All kinds of psychological problems can be changed and fixed. Depression will lift from you and flee, because you are not allowing the earth realm to define who you are! Hear me; one good thought from God could liberate you more than any psychologist can! Do hear me! – If you are reading this book and are being attacked by depression, low self-esteem or whatever else the enemy might be throwing at you; please take hold of this revelation in your spirit and in your mind – *we are Citizens of Heaven*, now; and just like the Philippians we are being changed from the inside daily so that we can function by Heaven's standards and values while currently walking in the earth!

Now tell me after reading and understanding all of this – can you walk the earth again and be brought down by people's opinion of you? *NO*. Could we walk around the earth without an identity not knowing who we are and living a completely defeated, depressed life? *NO*. Our thoughts about ourselves must go up and climb up to where He is. It is a Heavenly, *upward call*. The Apostle Paul goes on to cue us into the reality of true maturity in Christ.

> "All of us who are *mature* should take such a view of things. And if on some point you think differently, that too God will make clear to you. Only let us live up to what we have already attained." [NIV Philippians 3:15-16 Italics Added]

When he speaks of *maturity* here, he refers to those who are pressing upward, those who have answered the Heavenly, *upward call*. These verses give us such powerful application for life – He is saying that once we begin to walk this way if there is any level of deficiency in our mentality then God will bring the adjustment. He goes on to say that while the ultimate goal is for us to lay hold of the prize of the mark of that *upward call*; one should not despise the small gains that you make along the way as you progress towards the ultimate! When you understand a principle then walk in it – to the degree that you understand, walk in it. This is a progressive walk and lifestyle! Do not go backwards.

Abraham's life provides us with such a tremendous metaphor for our own lives and journey; and as such it would be wise for us to briefly look at this in order to bring greater clarity to our position. As we read Hebrews 11:8-14 there are some similarities to our lives and what the Apostle Paul was conveying in his letters.

> "By faith Abraham obeyed when he was called to go out to the place which he would receive as an inheritance. And he went out, not knowing where he was going. 9 By faith he dwelt in the land of promise as in a foreign country, dwelling in tents with Isaac and Jacob, the heirs with him of the same promise; 10 for he waited for the city which has foundations, whose builder and maker is God. 11 By faith Sarah herself also received strength to conceive seed, and she bore a child when she was past the age, because she judged Him faithful who had promised. 12 Therefore from one man, and him as good as dead, were born as many as the stars of the sky in multitude--innumerable as the sand which is by the seashore. 13 These all died in faith, not having received the promises, but having seen them afar off were assured of them, embraced them and confessed that they were strangers and pilgrims on the earth.

14 For those who say such things declare plainly that they seek a homeland."

- He knew that he was a stranger or an alien.
- He lived in tents not putting down permanent roots in the earth system.
- He looked for that permanent city whose builder and maker was God – this is an apostolic mentality.
- He had a concept of Paul's teaching to the Saints at Philippi where they were Romans by decree, living in a Grecian culture.

Abraham, the father of faith began confessing that they were pilgrims and strangers in the earth. He embraced that which was far off and not earthly [because for all intents and purposes, they were in the Promised Land]. He knew that the Promised Land was not the real thing but only an allegory and that Heaven was the real deal!

When you begin to function like this upon the earth some people will call you arrogant. But I tell you this, knowledge and understanding is the difference between boldness and arrogance, between cockiness and confidence, between faith and fantasy. This is why the early Apostles had to pray for boldness to live this way upon the earth as Citizens of Heaven! Not only are we Citizens of Heaven; we are also called to be Ambassadors of Christ.

We Are Ambassadors Of Christ – 2 Corinthians 5:20
In essence there are Embassies of Heaven set up all over planet Earth; they are known as Churches and Ministries. Your home, your business, your family, etc are all embassies of Heaven and they carry out business on behalf of the Kingdom of God in the earth! – Hallelujah!

Do you understand the power of an embassy? For example the American Embassy in downtown Vancouver, BC where I live does not come under the jurisdiction of Canadian law even though it occupies physical space on Canadian soil. It functions by American law and all its officers' function by the laws of America and not the laws of Canada. In like manner the Canadian Embassy in the US does not come under US law. There is also something called Diplomatic Immunity; which [37]is a form of legal immunity and a policy held between governments, which ensures that diplomats are given safe passage and are considered not susceptible to lawsuit or prosecution under the host country's laws [although they can be expelled.] By the same token, we do not come under the laws of the earth realm, once we are under the protection and jurisdiction of the Embassy from Heaven!

Before closing this writing, I would like for us to spend a few moments re-emphasising this fact. In doing so let us briefly revisit Jesus' discourse with His disciples in Matthew 16:13-19! Here we see Jesus mentioning the Church for the very first time and it is in conjunction with the Kingdom... As you would realize, He chose to reveal this in the city of Philippi, which we established was a very important city...

> "When Jesus came into the region of Caesarea Philippi, He asked His disciples, saying, "Who do men say that I, the Son of Man, am?" [14] So they said, "Some *say* John the Baptist, some Elijah, and others Jeremiah or one of the prophets." [15] He said to them, "But who do you say that I am?" [16] Simon Peter answered and said, "You are the Christ, the Son of the living God." [17] Jesus answered and said to him, "Blessed are you, Simon

---

[37] Taken from Wikipedia's website.

Bar-Jonah, for flesh and blood has not revealed *this* to you, but My Father who is in heaven. ¹⁸ And I also say to you that you are Peter, and on this rock I will build My church, and the gates of Hades shall not prevail against it. ¹⁹ And I will give you the keys of the kingdom of heaven, and whatever you bind on earth will be bound in heaven, and whatever you loose on earth will be loosed in heaven."

In essence He told them that while they walked the face of the earth that they were to function by Heaven's standards. He also revealed to them that they were to understand and walk in their rights and privileges as a Citizen of the Kingdom of Heaven.

In like manner we are to function and operate the very same way as Citizens of the Kingdom of God. And just like a natural embassy is a fort or protected place in the earth, likewise the Church—the *Fortress Church* – every local church that is birth and planted by the Lord is an Embassy of the Kingdom of Heaven and they are all well protected!

☞ CHAPTER 6

THE CHURCH AT EPHESUS

The New Testament paints a vivid picture of the Church with its rich descriptions of the Church, as it should be. The church at Ephesus was undoubtedly blessed from the letters that Apostle Paul wrote to them as he painted such revelatory pictures of the Church to them. It would serve well for us to explore these descriptions, as they would further assist in our understanding of the Church that Jesus Christ said He would build.

The Church at Ephesus presents to us another great description of the *"Fortress Church!"* It was also the One commended by the Lord for testing or trying those who claim to be Apostles and found some of them to be liars. I find this particularly interesting as it was to the Church at Ephesus that the Apostle Paul wrote the most comprehensive and detailed understanding of the Church of Jesus Christ, which I would like to briefly explore. He clearly described seven dimensions or aspects of what the Church of Jesus Christ is:

1. His Assembly [Ephesians 1:22 – YLT]
2. His Body [Ephesians 1:23]
3. His Workmanship or Masterpiece [Ephesians 2:10]
4. His Household or Family [Ephesians 2:18-19]
5. His Building or Temple [Ephesians 2:20-22]
6. His Bride or Wife [Ephesians 5:25-32]
7. His Army [Ephesians 6:10-13]

Before broaching the subject of these seven dimensions of the Church, it would be fitting for us to have a brief look at the city where this local church was located.

Ephesus was a luxurious and splendid eastern city but witchcraft with its black arts and idolatrous superstitions of the Orient were at the centre core. Ephesus could well be called "superstition city" as its people lived in a superstitious atmosphere. The Ephesians worshipped the Asiatic goddess Diana and its supreme glory was the temple of Artemis or Diana, one of the Seven Wonders of the World, which made the city famous. Not only at Ephesus, but throughout all of Asia and the then known world, the multi-breasted statue of Diana was worshipped as the goddess of virginity and motherhood from the outset and this veneration of her as the great has transcended from this pagan god over into the veneration of Mary as a religious force among the members of the Roman Catholic church.

Ephesus was the capital of pro-consular Asia, about 40 miles SE of Smyrna and was a wealthy metropolis during Apostle Paul's day. The word Ephesus means "desirable" and this was reflected in the fact that it was called "The Treasure House of Asia." Ephesus was a proud, rich, and busy port, known as the market of Asia Minor and in those days trade followed the river valleys and Ephesus stood at the mouth of the Cayster commanding the richest hinterland in Asia Minor.

Under the shadow of the temple of Artemis [Diana], ghostly priests and miracle workers abounded. Between the occult worship of Artemis and the widespread practice of magic, the city was preoccupied with the black arts. The worship of Artemis included shameless and vile practices such as prostitution and mutilation in the rituals. This made the residents easy prey to false magicians and vulnerable to demonic penetration. There were also the famous charms and spells called "Ephesians' Letters" that guaranteed to bring protection on journeys, children to the childless, and success in love or business. With this fame, people from all over the world came to Ephesus to buy these magic parchments, which they wore as amulets and charms. This was the backdrop of demonic activity and darkness that the Lord sent Apostle Paul in to establish the Ephesians' church.

The letter of Paul to the Ephesians was written during his imprisonment at Rome and was carried by Tychicus on his journey to Asia. This was a church that had been born in revival. In Acts Chapters 18-20, we read of how Paul came to Ephesus and preached for three months in the synagogue. Although he was greatly opposed, God did a great work in the city. We read in Acts 19:20, *"So mightily grew the Word of God and prevailed."*

The church at Ephesus is the first of the seven candlesticks of the apocalypse. The church at Ephesus was more than a building where people gathered. It was a body of Believers that worshipped on the first day of the week and worked the rest of the week. The word *"labour"* describes the kind of working congregation they were. The word describes "toiling to the point of exhaustion." It speaks of a "strenuous and exhausting labour." They were such hard workers; they were completely exhausting themselves in the work of Lord. The Believers in Ephesus worked themselves to the state of exhaustion for the sake of Jesus. Their labour cost them something...

Also, remember at that time there were no church buildings or denominations so the Believers met in halls or homes or wherever they could. There was not one great central temple where they all met. Several small congregations under separate Eldership made up the Ephesians' church; but the letter is addressed to "The church at Ephesus" – one church with many congregations.

This was the backdrop from which the Apostle Paul so masterfully and explicitly expounded and explained the Church that Jesus Christ was building and the Church He wanted to see manifest in the church at Ephesus.

As one journeys through the verses of the letter to the Ephesians we find several [38]descriptions of the Church, which reveals the multi-faceted nature of the Church that Jesus Christ is building. The first of these descriptions is in the fact that the Church is God's Assembly or Ecclesia!

> "And God placed all things under his feet and appointed him to be head over everything for the church..." [Ephesians 1:22]

The Church As God's Assembly Or Ecclesia:
The Greek word for church here is ecclesia, which is derived from a verb that means, "to call out". The idea is being that of a smaller group of people that is called out from a larger group. It also refers to a smaller group called out for a specific purpose; and applies to the Church being called out from the world...

From this we can say that the Church has been called out of the world through faith in Jesus Christ for a special purpose

---

[38] The seven pictures or descriptions of the Church is borrowed from the author's gleaning from the book "Rediscovering God's Church" masterfully written by the late Derek Prince and published by Whitaker House; and used by permission.

of God! Scripture was originally written in secular Greek, the language of the day. The word ecclesia carried the very specific meaning of governmental assembly.

If we are called out, we can deduce that the Church is not to be an insular organisation more concerned with its image and not at all concerned with life issues, which surround it. No, the Church is God's Governmental Assembly in the earth. The Church is here to conduct the affairs of God's Kingdom on earth. When Jesus revealed to the early Apostles that He had His Assembly of "called out ones" or His Kingdom Ecclesia; He was telling them that just as the Romans had their senate or ecclesia; He had His. Jesus did all that was required of Him to prepare the Apostles for the building work that would follow. Jesus would depart for heaven, and these Apostles were to become the initial builders of the Church – as recorded by Matthew.

> "And I tell you that you are Peter, and on this rock I will build my church, and the gates of Hades will not overcome it. 19 I will give you the keys of the kingdom of heaven; whatever you bind on earth will be bound in heaven, and whatever you loose on earth will be loosed in heaven." [Matthew 16:18-19]

> "Then the eleven disciples left for Galilee, going to the mountain where Jesus had said they would find him. 17 There they met him and worshiped him-but some of them weren't sure it really was Jesus! 18 He told his disciples, "I have been given all authority in heaven and earth. 19 Therefore go and make disciples in all the nations, baptizing them into the name of the Father and of the Son and of the Holy Spirit, 20 and then teach these new disciples to obey all the commands I have given you; and be sure of this-that I am with you always, even to the end of the

world." [TLB Matthew 28:16-20]

From this we see that God has deposited much governmental authority in His Assembly – both local and global – [not the individual]!

The next description that we read of the Church is that of being the Body of Jesus Christ!

> "And God placed all things under his feet and appointed him to be head over everything for the church, 23 which is his body, the fullness of him who fills everything in every way." [Ephesians 1:22-23]

The Body of Jesus Christ:
First off let me say this – we relate to the world we live in through our bodies. It is in a body that we get things done in the world of time and space. That's why when God wanted to redeem the world back to Himself; He gave Jesus Christ a Body to come to earth in order to function. Similarly Jesus Christ relates to the world through us – His Body [the Church].

Here is how the writer of Hebrews said it:

> "Therefore, when Christ came into the world, he said: "Sacrifice and offering you did not desire, but a body you prepared for me; 6 with burnt offerings and sin offerings you were not pleased. 7 Then I said, `Here I am-it is written about me in the scroll-I have come to do your will, O God.'" [Hebrews 10:5-7]

This passage of Scripture is very clear and comes in two parts:

1. A Body You prepared for Me.
2. To do Your Will O God.

This tells us that the function of the Body that was prepared for Jesus Christ was so that He could do the Will of God in the earth!

However, we can take this one step further to see the two-fold aspect of Jesus Christ's Body:

1. His Physical, Natural Body that became the Sacrifice for the sins of the entire world, on the Cross!

2. His Spiritual Body – the Church [the combination of all Born-again Believers in the earth] continues to do God's Will in the earth!

So as the Body of Jesus Christ in the earth, every Born-again Believer has a part in the Body. The Bible goes on to reveal that the Head of the Body is indeed Jesus Christ – both of the Universal Church and the local church. It also goes on to make a powerful statement when it says, "the Head cannot say to the feet, I have no need of you" [1 Corinthians 12:21]. So when the Believer is feeling that they are of little consequence to the functioning of the Church, this passage assures us that it does not matter where or what place one has in the Body, that we are all needed!

For emphasis, on what we just read, we will read what Apostle Paul wrote to the Church at Corinth concerning the Body:

> "Now the body is not made up of one part but of many. 15 If the foot should say, "Because I am not a hand, I do not belong to the body," it would not for that reason cease to be part of the body. 16 And if the ear should say, "Because I am not an eye, I do not belong to the body," it would not for that reason cease to be part of the body. 17 If the whole body were an eye, where would the sense of hearing be? If the whole body were an ear, where would the sense

of smell be? 18 But in fact God has arranged the parts in the body, every one of them, just as he wanted them to be. 19 If they were all one part, where would the body be? 20 As it is, there are many parts, but one body. 21 The eye cannot say to the hand, "I don't need you!" And the head cannot say to the feet, "I don't need you!" 22 On the contrary, those parts of the body that seem to be weaker are indispensable, 23 and the parts that we think are less honourable we treat with special honour. And the parts that are unpresentable are treated with special modesty, 24 while our presentable parts need no special treatment. But God has combined the members of the body and has given greater honour to the parts that lacked it, 25 so that there should be no division in the body, but that its parts should have equal concern for each other. 26 If one part suffers, every part suffers with it; if one part is honoured, every part rejoices with it. 27 Now you are the body of Christ, and each one of you is a part of it." [1 Corinthians 12:14-28]

Apostle Paul goes on to paint for us a beautiful picture of The Complete Body:

"Instead, speaking the truth in love, we will in all things grow up into him who is the Head, that is, Christ. 16 From him the whole body, *joined and held together by every supporting ligament*, grows and builds itself up in love, as each part does its work." [Italics Added Ephesians 4:16]

Guided by the Holy Spirit, here the Apostle Paul reveals to us the dynamics of the Body of Christ:

- That just as with the human body, in the Church, there is many joints and ligaments that hold the body intact.

- That as a body we are one in Christ
- That as we are held together in this single, organic unity, the Body builds itself up.
- That in order for this building up to occur, the Body depends on each part to do its work.
- This implies that one unhealthy part affects the health of the rest of the Body. If gangrene sets into your little finger, it can poison the whole body, which can result in death.

Apostle Paul further declares:

"Let no one cheat you of your reward, taking delight in false humility and worship of angels, intruding into those things which he has not seen, vainly puffed up by his fleshly mind, 19 and not holding fast *to the Head, from whom all the body, nourished and knit together by joints and ligaments, grows with the increase that is from God.*" [Italics Added Colossians 2:18-19]

Very Important To Understand:
We do not get our needs met through the Head alone; but through the network of joints and ligaments throughout the Body, which are all linked in various ways to the Head!

Joints:
Just as joints in the human body allow for bending and contortion that an utterly stiff body without joints would not have, in the spiritual relationship of the Body, joints are the interrelationships between the various members of the Body, through which God's supply comes!

Ligaments:
The purpose of having ligaments is to hold the skeleton to-

gether in a normal alignment – ligaments prevent abnormal movements. However, when too much force is applied to a ligament, the ligaments can be stretched or torn. Hence ligaments strengthen the joints and protect them. In the spiritual sense, a ligament is committed, covenant love – love that is committed to another person, commitment that says through thick and thin, we stick together. For example; the kind of love that a man has to his wife – [for better, for worse; in sickness and in health]!!!

Ephesians 2:10 reveals that the Church is God's Workmanship or Masterpiece according to the ISV translation!

> "For we are God's workmanship, created in Christ Jesus to do good works, which God prepared in advance for us to do."

> "For we are his masterpiece, created in Christ Jesus for good works that God prepared long ago to be our way of life." [ISV]

The Church As God's Workmanship/Masterpiece
The Greek word poiema that is translated into our English word workmanship does not really bring out the real significance of the word. However, poiema comes from the Latin poema, from which we get the English word *Poem*! So, in essence this word for workmanship is taken from a word that is descriptive of the arts and creativity so we could then translate Ephesians 2:10 to say that – "We are God's creative Masterpiece..."

Truly this is a humbling thought that the Creator of the universe and all that is in it would choose people like you and me to make up *His Creative Masterpiece*... The concept of a masterpiece lends to the idea that there must be other pieces in the puzzle. As such we can conclude that when the

Church is placed alongside everything that God has created – the Church stands out far and above everything else!

Poetry is artistry with words. It is the blending together of words to evoke a picture, make an impression, or to create an impact! In essence, each word in a poem must be the precise word set in just the right place and perfectly related to the other words around it. In the same way God wants to make us [the local church and also the Universal Church] collectively into a poem, with each one of us being carefully selected and placed in the right position in relation to all the others around us!

Why is He doing this? – We are God's Poem! We are His Creative Masterpiece – Ephesians 3:10 answers that question: "His intent was that now, through the church, the manifold wisdom of God should be made known to the rulers and authorities in the heavenly realms…"

This revelation was very vital for the church at Ephesus as it was being built and functioned in the heartland of demonic activity. Witchcraft and sorcery and every demonic work under the sun were practiced there. As a matter of fact witchcraft and sorcery was the mainstay of that region's economy. And still the church flourished in spite of its surrounding demonic influence. And Apostle Paul was saying to them that as the church functioned the way that Jesus Christ intended it would absolutely showcase God's wisdom for all to see!

This picture painted of the Church is absolutely breathtaking and quite astonishing to say the least. Paul reveals to us by the Holy Spirit that God chose us – His redeemed people, to demonstrate His manifold [multi-faceted or many-sided] wisdom to the entire universe – in time and space and in eternity – and to the unseen heavenly realms! So we the Church as His Masterpiece contains His Manifold Wisdom – we, the Church of Jesus Christ are the ones God is using to confound principality and powers – not angels, but we the Redeemed!!!

Where did God get the material for His greatest Masterpiece? – He formed it from His Church! Yes, the material is the Church made up of former sinners, who He bought back from the devil with the Precious Blood of His Son...

Ephesians 2:10 reveal to us that we were created to do good works, well in advance by God... We were not created to be ornaments; no, we were created to be useful to the Lord...

The Church As The Family of God:

> "It is through Christ that all of us, Jews and Gentiles, are able to come in the one Spirit into the presence of the Father. (19) So then, you Gentiles are not foreigners or strangers any longer; you are now citizens together with God's people and members of the family of God." [GNB Ephesians 2:18-19]

As we explore the entirety of the New Testament; God's people are very seldom referred to by the title Christians or even Believers. The first recorded use of the term "Christian" is found in the New Testament, in Acts 11:26, which states "...in Antioch the disciples were first called Christians." The second mention of the term follows in Acts 26:28, where Herod Agrippa II replies to Paul the Apostle, "Do you think that in such a short time you can persuade me to be a Christian?" The third and final New Testament reference to the term is in 1 Peter 4:16, which exhorts Believers, "...if you suffer as a Christian, do not be ashamed, but praise God that you bear that name". [Wikipedia] However, the most common collective title used for Christians is "brothers" which emphasizes the fact that we are members in one spiritual family. Remember that we have become members of God's Family [Household] because of Christ's sacrifice, which gained us access because of His relationship to the Father! God's Family is determined by relationship to the Father...

In Greek the word used for family is patria and is derived from the word that is used for father – pater. Apostle Paul puts it beautifully in the following reference:

> "For this reason I bow my knees to the Father of our Lord Jesus Christ, 15 from whom the whole family in heaven and earth is named..." [Ephesians 3:14-15]

There is a direct play on words "Father and Family" – showing that family comes from fatherhood. This is further clarified in:

> "For it was fitting for Him, for whom are all things and by whom are all things, in *bringing many sons to glory*, to make the captain of their salvation perfect through sufferings. 11 For *both He who sanctifies and those who are being sanctified are all of one, for which reason He is not ashamed to call them brethren*, 12 saying: "I will declare Your name *to My brethren; In the midst of the assembly* I will sing praise to You." [Hebrews 2:10-12 Italics Added]

There is a simple yet powerful revelation contained in this passage: God has made us His sons through Jesus, and Jesus Himself is the Only Begotten Son, of God the Father. Because of this fact, Jesus acknowledges us as His brothers – because of our relationship to the Father. Remember that Jesus never did anything without His Father's leading and direction; and as such Jesus never called us "brothers" until He heard His Father calls us "sons". Once His Father referred to us as His sons, then Jesus acknowledged us as His brothers.

The Idea of A Shared Life-Source:
When we all share the same life-source then we are members of the same family. The Father is the life-source of every family both in Heaven and on earth – [we cannot have a family without a father being the life-source as he carries the sperm]!

Remember that a family in not a denomination or a label, nor is it an organisation or institution. A family is a family because it has the same life-source!!!

Jesus aptly describes or exemplified the awesome relationships within the Family of God by the opening words of what some call the Lord's Prayer.

> "In this manner, therefore, pray: Our Father in heaven, Hallowed be Your name." [Matthew 6:9]

Understanding the Fatherhood of God is essential to our growth and effective life on the earth... Jesus made this very clear in His powerful address in the following reference:

> "Thomas said to Him, "Lord, we do not know where You are going, and how can we know the way?" 6 Jesus said to him, "I am the way, the truth, and the life. No one comes to the Father except through Me. 7 "If you had known Me, you would have known My Father also; and from now on you know Him and have seen Him." 8 Philip said to Him, "Lord, show us the Father, and it is sufficient for us." 9 Jesus said to him, "Have I been with you so long, and yet you have

not known Me, Philip? He who has seen Me has seen the Father; so how can you say, 'Show us the Father'? 10 Do you not believe that I am in the Father, and the Father in Me? The words that I speak to you I do not speak on My own authority; but the Father who dwells in Me does the works." [John 14:5-10]

Jesus in this address keeps referring to His Father and this was summed up in this statement when He said: "I am the way, the truth, and the life. No one comes to the Father except through Me."

However, most times when this Scripture is quoted folks stop short and only say that "Jesus is the way, the truth, and the life", but that is not the end of the quote.

A way is meaningless unless it leads somewhere – where does Jesus [the Way] lead us? – To the Father! We have not fulfilled the purpose of God if we merely find the way – we need to know the destination! Remember that the primary mission of Jesus Christ was not to bring us unto Himself, but to bring us to the Father!

Remember – "For it was fitting for Him, for whom are all things and by whom are all things, *in bringing many sons to glory*, to make the captain of their salvation perfect through sufferings." [Hebrews 2:10 Italics Added]

The Church is indeed a close-knit Family of Brothers and Sisters: Of the different New Testament terms used to describe the nature of the Church, this is the one most frequently used.

Robert Banks, a prominent leader in the worldwide home-church movement, makes this observation in his book, *Paul's Idea of Community*:

"Although in recent years Paul's metaphors for community

have been subjected to quite intense study, especially his description of it as a "body," his application to it of "household" or "family" terminology has all too often been overlooked or only mentioned in passing.

Banks further comments on the frequency and significance of these familial expressions: So numerous are these, and so frequently do they appear, that the comparison of the Christian community with a "family" must be regarded as the most significant metaphorical usage of all... More than any of the other images utilized by Paul, it reveals the essence of his thinking about community.

The local Christian church then, is to be a close-knit family of brothers and sisters. Brotherliness also provided a key guiding principle for the management of relationships between Christians [Romans 14:15, 21; 1 Corinthians 6:8; 8:11-13; 2 Thessalonians 3:14, 15; Philemon 15-16; James 4:11]. Jesus insisted that His followers were true brothers and sisters and that none among them should act like the rabbis of His day who elevated themselves above their fellow countrymen":

> "But they do all their deeds to be noticed by men; for they broaden their phylacteries, and lengthen the tassels of their garments. And they love the place of honour at banquets, and the chief seats in the synagogues, and respectful greetings in the market places, and being called by men, Rabbi. *But do not be called Rabbi*; for One is your Teacher, and *you are all brothers.*" [Matthew 23:5-8 Italics Added]

Again the essential feature of the picture of the Church as God's Family is the fact that we have one shared life-source. God our Father in Heaven is the life-source of His entire family-His Church. The fact that we all share the same life-source, we all share a common life is what binds us together and not denominations or doctrines or labels...

The Church as The Temple Of God:

> "...built on the foundation of the apostles and prophets, with Christ Jesus himself as the chief cornerstone. 21 In him the whole building is joined together and rises to become a holy temple in the Lord. 22 And in him you too are being built together to become a dwelling place in which God lives by his Spirit." [Ephesians 2:20-21]

In Hebrew the word for house is beit and carries the concept of a home or family. As a matter of fact it is directly connected to the Hebrew word that translates "to build"! So in Hebrew thinking there is a close connection between family and building. The word they used to translate "house" was not used to describe a dwelling place but rather a family or people. As a matter of fact we can notice the emphasis on building in the passage – *built, building, temple, built, dwelling place...* Five times, the thought is brought out here.

God has always required His people to provide Him with a dwelling place. When God delivered the Israelites out of Egypt and brought them first to Mt. Sinai and gave them His Covenant one of the first things that He required was for them to build Him a Tabernacle. This Tent became the dwelling place for His Manifested Presence – His Shekinah Glory – and this Presence travelled with the Israelites all the way through the wilderness.

When He brought them into the Promised Land He gave them instructions to build Him a Temple in Jerusalem. King Solomon eventually built Him an elaborate Temple for His Presence to dwell. Through their idolatry and disobedience, the Temple was eventually destroyed by the Babylonians. God then had mercy on them and granted them restoration from Babylon and one of their first assignments was to rebuild the Temple.

Now these temples or tabernacles were only patterns of the Church as was spoken by Stephen in the Book of Acts:

> "However, the Most High does not live in houses made by men. As the prophet says: 49 "Heaven is my throne, and the earth is my footstool. What kind of house will you build for me? says the Lord. Or where will my resting place be? 50 Has not my hand made all these things?" [Acts 7:48-50]

Most Believers know this, but I will still say it – no matter how beautiful the edifice is we build even with the best of natural materials, it is not the final Dwelling Place for the Lord!!! The truth is that His Temple is to be constructed with People! It is not being constructed with the most valuable materials on the planet like diamonds, gold, silver or marble but with *people*!!! This truth is clearly brought out in the following passage:

> "By the grace God has given me, I laid a foundation as an expert builder, and someone else is building on it. But each one should be careful how he builds. 11 For no one can lay any foundation other than the one already laid, which is Jesus Christ. 12 If any man builds on this foundation using gold, silver, costly stones, wood, hay or straw, 13 his work will be shown for what it is, because the Day will bring it to light. It will be revealed with fire, and the fire will test the quality of each man's work. 14 If what he has built survives, he will receive his reward. 15 If it is burned up, he will suffer loss; he himself will be

saved, but only as one escaping through the flames."
[1 Corinthians 3:10-15]

There are two types of buildings you can erect – those that will stand the test and those that will not! You can build with wood, hay or straw, which is in great quantity, or you can build with precious stones, which are not in great quantity and are much harder to come by. This particular passage is talking about our contribution in the service of God's Temple – it is going to have to stand the test of fire. We are reminded of the following!

> "For we must all appear before the judgment seat of Christ, that each one may receive what is due him for the things done while in the body, whether good or bad." [2 Corinthians 5:10]

This is not speaking about the judgement of the world and sinners; or of salvation or condemnation; for there is no condemnation to those who are in Christ [Romans 8:1]. This is not speaking about the destiny of souls, but it is speaking about the work that we have done in the House of God.

When dealing with the Church as the Temple of God there is always a warning against defiling it – both the Collective and the Individual Temple. Paul had to warn the Corinthian Believers about this:

> "Don't you know that you yourselves are God's temple and that God's Spirit lives in you? 17 If anyone destroys God's temple, God will destroy him; for God's temple is sacred, and you are that temple."
> [1 Corinthians 3:16-17]

> "Do you not know that your body is a temple of the Holy Spirit, who is in you, whom you have received

from God? You are not your own; 20 you were bought at a price. Therefore honour God with your body." [1 Corinthians 6:19-20]

Every Believer has the privilege of providing his/her own physical body to the Holy Spirit as a temple to dwell in. God has redeemed our bodies so that it might be a temple for His Spirit!!! Once again we are warned to be careful that we do not defile or destroy the temple – whether the Collective or Individual Temple – we are required to take care of it and preserve it in purity!

> "Do not be yoked together with unbelievers. For what do righteousness and wickedness have in common? Or what fellowship can light have with darkness? 15 What harmony is there between Christ and Belial? What does a believer have in common with an unbeliever? 16 What agreement is there between the temple of God and idols? For we are the temple of the living God. As God has said: "I will live with them and walk among them, and I will be their God, and they will be my people." [2 Corinthians 6:14-16]

This passage is speaking about the Collective Temple:
As the Temple of God we do not "go to Church" we are the Church. Wherever we gather we are the Church. He lives in us, walks in us and functions in us – we are His Temple.

The Temple Is Made Of Living Stones:

> "As you come to him, the living Stone-rejected by men but chosen by God and precious to him- 5 you also, like living stones, are being built into a spiritual house to be a holy priesthood, offering spiritual sacrifices acceptable to God through Jesus Christ." [1 Peter 2:4-5]

You and I and every Born-Again, Spirit-Filled Believer are the

Living Stones building the Eternal House in which God would dwell!

The Church As The Bride Of Jesus Christ:

> "Husbands, love your wives, just as Christ loved the church and gave himself up for her 26 to make her holy, cleansing her by the washing with water through the word, 27 and to present her to himself as a radiant church, without stain or wrinkle or any other blemish, but holy and blameless." 28 In this same way, husbands ought to love their wives as their own bodies. He who loves his wife loves himself. 29 After all, no one ever hated his own body, but he feeds and cares for it, just as Christ does the church- 30 for we are members of his body. 31 "For this reason a man will leave his father and mother and be united to his wife, and the two will become one flesh." 32 This is a profound mystery-but I am talking about Christ and the church. [Ephesians 5:25-32 Italics Added]

Although the word Bride is not used in the Scripture in regards to the Church the implication is certain! Apostle Paul began this exaltation towards husbands and their treatment of their wives; he declared that their relationship must be one of love, devotion and care. All that was sound and practical advice and much needed in today's world and I dare say the North American church, which is rife with so many divorces and rampant infidelity! However, he was after a much deeper truth and it is the fact that the husband/wife relationship is patterned after the relationship of Jesus Christ and His Church.

Paul even added that it was a *profound mystery*: – yes it is indeed a profound mystery as no human mind could adequately comprehend this: that Jesus Christ is the Bridegroom and the

Church is His Bride! Now to fully understand this we need to take a brief look at the original creation [Adam and Eve in particular], which I believe overshadows this union between Christ and His Church [Bride].

An interesting feature of creation is the fact that before Adam appeared on the scene God created everything that he would need before hand; the earth, the planets, all the heavenly bodies, the vegetation, the animals, the weather, etc... However, there was only one thing missing for Adam and that was a mate! This was not a mistake on God's part. I believe that He wanted Adam to understand what it meant to long for personal fellowship with one of his own kind; another human being! The animals and everything else surrounding him could not provide that for him as he was created with the need for human fellowship!

God allowed Adam to experience the lack of that fellowship in order for him to be aware of his need for a mate – and then the Lord saw that it was not good for man to be alone and brought forth Eve unto the scene:

> "The LORD God said, "*It is not good for the man to be alone [Adam had to be manifesting his aloneness]. I will make a helper suitable for him.*" 19 Now the LORD God had formed out of the ground all the beasts of the field and all the birds of the air. He brought them to the man to see what he would name them; and whatever the man called each living creature, that was its name. 20 So the man gave names to all the livestock, the birds of the air and all the beasts of the field. But for Adam no suitable helper was found. 21 So the LORD God caused the man to fall into a deep sleep; and while he was sleeping, he took one of the man's ribs and closed up the place with flesh. 22 Then the LORD God made a

woman from the rib he had taken out of the man, and he brought her to the man. 23 The man said, "This is now bone of my bones and flesh of my flesh; she shall be called `woman,' for she was taken out of man." [Genesis 2:18, 21-23 Italics Added]

This is one the most powerful reasons for marriage; the fact that God places a tremendous emphasis on it. Marriage plays a central part in the whole of creation. Life began with a marriage and life, as we know it will end with a Marriage. The same way God formed a wife for Adam He is forming a Bride [the Church] for His Son. Remember that Jesus when He was on the Cross they pierced His side [John 19:31-34; I believe that was a type of the first Adam when his rib was taken out in order to create Eve].

There is going to be a marriage – It is a Spiritual Marriage called the Marriage Supper of the Lamb:

"I saw the Holy City, the New Jerusalem, coming down out of heaven from God, *prepared as a bride beautifully dressed for her husband.* 3 And I heard a loud voice from the throne saying, "Now the dwelling of God is with men, and he will live with them. They will be his people, and God himself will be with them and be their God... 9 One of the seven angels who had the seven bowls full of the seven last plagues came and said to me, "*Come, I will show you the bride, the wife of the Lamb.*" 10 And he carried me away in the Spirit to a mountain great and high, and showed me the Holy City, Jerusalem, coming down out of heaven from God. 11 It shone with the glory of God, and its brilliance was like that of a very precious jewel, like a jasper, clear as crystal." [Revelation 21:2-3, 9-11 Italics Added]

The Bride of Jesus Christ Makes Herself Ready:
Human history as we now know it will come to an end one

day and its climax will be the Marriage of the Church [The Bride] to Jesus Christ [The Bridegroom]!

> "Then I heard what sounded like a great multitude, like the roar of rushing waters and like loud peals of thunder, shouting: "Hallelujah! For our Lord God Almighty reigns. 7 Let us rejoice and be glad and give him glory! For the wedding of the Lamb has come, and his bride has made herself ready. 8 Fine linen, bright and clean, was given her to wear." [Fine linen stands for the righteous acts of the saints.]" [Revelation 19:6-8]

To me this is very interesting; the Marriage of the Church to Jesus Christ will be a time of great rejoicing but what stands out to me is the fact the Bible declares that it is the Bride who has made Herself ready. She prepares Her own clothing and it clearly states that the clothing [fine linen] stands for the *righteous acts* or righteousness of the Saints!

In Greek there are two different words used for righteousness:

The first word is dikaiosune and it means – righteousness in the abstract. For example when we get saved God's Righteousness is imputed or deposited into us [not because of anything that we have done]; we are made righteous because of the fact that Jesus Christ is Righteous!

The second word is dikaioma and it means – righteousness in action, righteousness that is worked out or literally translated "acts of righteousness" – that is, what we have done.

The word for righteousness used in Revelation is dikaioma, so the Bride has made Herself ready, how? By the dikaiomata [righteous acts] of the Saints! I also find this interesting because in every culture that I have either experienced or read about, the bridegroom never prepares the bride for marriage – the bride always prepares herself!

"For the wedding of the Lamb has come, and his bride has made herself ready." – We have to make ourselves ready, by our acts of righteousness; there is just *no other way*!

For us to fully understand the implications of what is being said here we need to be acquainted with some basic principles of marriage from a Jewish perspective [during the time of this writing].

Basically there were two ceremonies:
First there is what is known as the betrothal – this is similar to our western custom of engagement.

The Second was the actual marriage ceremony, which was then followed by the physical union between the man and his bride.

In Hebrew custom betrothal was a very sacred, binding covenant agreement between a man and a woman. Although they still lived apart and did not come together in a physical union or relationship, the woman was bound to the man by covenant. If at any time she broke that covenant or betrothal or engagement to marry someone else, or if she participated in sexual relations with another man, she was actually treated as an adulteress and a bill of divorce officially nullified the covenant. That is how serious the betrothal commitment was!

Betrothed couples were regarded legally as husband and wife, even before their wedding ceremony and physical union. And it is such with Jesus Christ and the Church in Her current state. The Church is the Bride in waiting or more accurately the Bride in preparation for Marriage; She is already betrothed and espoused to Jesus Christ and His Father has already set the date. Although the Marriage Ceremony has not yet taken place we are to remain faithful to Him. As a matter of fact our loyalty will be tested during this period before the Ceremony takes place

Have you ever really noticed a young lady who is truly in love and is engaged? Her face beams and glows whenever she is around the man that she is in love with [her husband to be] or whenever she speaks about him to anyone. The mere mention of his name brings a smile! In essence she is radiant. This is how the Lord God expects us to be. As a matter of fact the bride to be who is truly in love with the one she is espoused to does not and will not have eyes for anyone else.

I love what the Apostle Paul said in the following passage:

> "For I am jealous for you with godly jealousy. For I have betrothed you to one husband, that I may present you as a chaste virgin to Christ. 3 But I fear, lest somehow, as the serpent deceived Eve by his craftiness, so your minds may be corrupted from the simplicity that is in Christ. 4 For if he who comes preaches another Jesus whom we have not preached, or if you receive a different spirit which you have not received, or a different gospel which you have not accepted–you may well put up with it!" [2 Corinthians 11:2-4]

Apostle Paul was saying: "I want you to be a Chaste Virgin when you eventually marry the Bridegroom." This passage is so beautiful and because it was revealed to the Corinthian Church who were comprised of a cavalcade of ex-sinners [prostitutes, adulterers, homosexuals, drunkards and the list can go on and on] by natural standards. The members of this church would be the least likely to be considered as chaste virgins given their illicit backgrounds. However, the Grace of God and the finished work of Jesus Christ by His shed Blood were able to cleanse and redeem them. In the sight of God they were declared to be a Chaste Virgin!

I tell you with all conviction that there are two groups in Christendom today; not two denominations, but two groups! One is the Bride of Christ and the other is the harlot system. The Bride will remain loyal to Jesus Christ the harlot will be seduced away.

The harlot:
> "Then one of the seven angels who had the seven bowls came and talked with me, saying to me, "Come, I will show you the judgment of the great harlot who sits on many waters, 2 with whom the kings of the earth committed fornication, and the inhabitants of the earth were made drunk with the wine of her fornication." 3 So he carried me away in the Spirit into the wilderness. And I saw a woman sitting on a scarlet beast which was full of names of blasphemy, having seven heads and ten horns. 4 The woman was arrayed in purple and scarlet, and adorned with gold and precious stones and pearls, having in her hand a golden cup full of abominations and the filthiness of her fornication. 5 And on her forehead a name was written: *Mystery, Babylon The Great, The Mother Of Harlots And Of The Abominations Of The Earth.* 6 I saw the woman, drunk with the blood of the saints and with the blood of the martyrs of Jesus. And when I saw her, I marvelled with great amazement." [Revelation 17:1-6 Italics Added]

The Bride of Jesus Christ:
> "Then one of the seven angels who had the seven

> bowls filled with the seven last plagues came to me and talked with me, saying, "Come, I will show you the bride, the Lamb's wife." 10 And he carried me away in the Spirit to a great and high mountain, and showed me the great city, the holy Jerusalem, descending out of heaven from God, 11 having the glory of God. Her light was like a most precious stone, like a jasper stone, clear as crystal." [Revelation 21:9-11]

These two groups are separated by their relationship to the Bridegroom Jesus Christ. We must closely guard our relationship to Christ and not be drawn away by activities that would defile us!

The Church as The Army Of God:
> "Finally, be strong in the Lord and in his mighty power. 11 Put on the full armour of God so that you can take your stand against the devil's schemes. 12 For our struggle is not against flesh and blood, but against the rulers, against the authorities, against the powers of this dark world and against the spiritual forces of evil in the heavenly realms. 13 Therefore put on the full armour of God, so that when the day of evil comes, you may be able to stand your ground, and after you have done everything, to stand." [Ephesians 6:10-13]

This final picture of the Church as the Army of God is such a contrast from the Church as The Bride of Christ! In this passage not only the concept of warfare is revealed but Apostle Paul also warns Believers that we will most certainly face battles. He encourages putting on the entire armour of God to be able to stand in "the evil day"; the day of affliction, testing and satanic pressures. It is obvious, what kind of person puts on armour? – A soldier! The picture painted here by Apostle Paul was closely based on the battle gear of the Roman legionary in his time of writing. The Church is being compared to a Roman legion, the most effective military unit of the ancient world – one that actually conquered most of the known world for the Roman Empire.

While the term "army" is not applied to the Church in the New Testament, the pages therein are filled with militaristic references and characterizations of Christians as soldiers.

For example:
"Endure hardship with us like a good soldier of Christ Jesus. [4]No one serving as a soldier gets involved in civilian affairs—he wants to please his commanding officer." [2 Timothy 2:3-4]

This passage is explicit: Christians are to serve as good soldiers of Jesus Christ the Anointed One. He is our Recruiter.

The Apostle Paul certainly thought of his Christian brothers as soldiers for in Philemon 1:2 he writes: "to Apphia our sister, to Archippus our fellow soldier and to the church that meets in your home."

Jesus Himself referenced the battle in: Matthew 10:34
"Do not think that I came to bring peace on the earth.
I did not come to bring peace but a sword."

The word army does not appear in New Testament Scripture but the concept is undeniable. We see from these passages that the Christians are part of a military body and need to be vigilant, ready and armed for war, just as the Nation of Israel in the Old Testament.

Ever since the dawn of creation there has been warfare

between God and satan; between God's forces and that of the devil. With the advent of Jesus Christ coming as the Messiah and Saviour of mankind, the warfare came out into the open. And now that we have Born-again, Spirit-filled Believers because of the finished work of Calvary, the warfare is now turned between us, and the forces of darkness and the devil.

Spiritual Weapons and Warfare
Since Apostle Paul warned us about the spiritual warfare involved in being a part of the Church it is necessary for us to understand the weapons and battlefield of this warfare. He writes to the Corinthian church about this warfare and gives us a clearer insight:

> "For though we walk in the flesh, we do not war according to the flesh. 4 For the weapons of our warfare are not carnal but mighty in God for pulling down strongholds, 5 casting down arguments and every high thing that exalts itself against the knowledge of God, bringing every thought into captivity to the obedience of Christ, 6 and being ready to punish all disobedience when your obedience is fulfilled." [2 Corinthians 10:3-5]

Apostle Paul clearly reveals to us by the Holy Spirit that we are at war in the spiritual realm and that this warfare is the mind of mankind. He is saying that satan has setup fortresses in the minds of men and that first of all we must have our minds cleansed before going on to deal with the minds of others!

The Church as the Army of God is revealed so that we could understand the victory that we have in Jesus Christ and to also reveal that He is a Man of war! Scriptures are clear that this is one of the many dimensions of the Nature of the God we are called to serve – He is a Mighty Man of war! Here are a few of those references to this dimension of God's Nature:

When the Children of Israel were delivered from the tyranny of Pharaoh and Egypt and set out on their journey to the Promised Land; the armies of Egypt decided to try one last attempt to destroy them. At one point the Children of Israel were confronted with an insurmountable situation; the Red Sea was before them and Pharaoh's army behind; with nowhere to go, God performed an awesome miracle of having the Red Sea parted for them to go over on dry land and then sealing back the sea to see the host of Pharaoh's army drowned in the sea! On the other side and fresh from that victory they began to sing this song:

> "Then Moses and the children of Israel sang this song to the LORD, and spoke, saying: "I will sing to the LORD, For He has triumphed gloriously! The horse and its rider He has thrown into the sea! " 2 The LORD is my strength and song, And He has become my salvation; He is my God, and I will praise Him; My father's God, and I will exalt Him. 3 *The LORD is a man of war*; The LORD is His name." [Exodus 15:1-3 Italics Added]

So to the Israelites He was revealed as a Man of war! The Psalmist David goes on to further reveal this to us in the following excerpt from Psalms 24:7-10

> "Lift up your heads, O you gates! And be lifted up, you everlasting doors! And the King of glory shall come in. 8 Who is this King of glory? The LORD strong and mighty, The LORD mighty in battle. 9 Lift up your heads, O you gates! Lift up, you everlasting doors! And the King of glory shall come in. 10 Who is this King of glory? *The LORD of hosts*, He is the King of glory." [Italics Added]

The Lord of Hosts!
David reveals to us that the King of glory is known as "*the Lord of hosts*"! This designation reveals the warfare nature of God; as this term was borrowed from the Hebrew language.

This was the title used for the Lord as Commander of an army organized for battle. The word *hosts* is derived from the Hebrew word *tsaba* and carries the following shades of meaning: host; military service; war; army; service; labour; forced labour; conflict. This word involves several inter-related ideas: a group; impetus; difficulty; and force. These ideas undergird the general concept of *service* which one does for or under a superior rather than for oneself. Tsaba is usually applied to military service but is sometimes used of work in general [*under or for a superior*].

So the Lord is raising up an Army known as His Church and He is the Commander of the Church leading us into a battle that He has already secured the victory for! For this reason the Apostle Paul told us to put on the entire armour of God. We cannot fight if we do not have on our armour. Before closing this chapter let us briefly explore the symbolism of the armour!

> "Stand firm then, with the belt of truth buckled around your waist, with the breastplate of righteousness in place, 15 and with your feet fitted with the readiness that comes from the gospel of peace. 16 In addition to all this, take up the shield of faith, with which you can extinguish all the flaming arrows of the evil one. 17 Take the helmet of salvation and the sword of the Spirit, which is the word of God. 18 And pray in the Spirit on all occasions with all kinds of prayers and requests.

With this in mind, be alert and always keep on praying for all the saints." [NIV Ephesians 6:14-18]

The Belt of Truth:
Soldiers in Paul's day wore belts to secure their clothing and hold weapons. The belt of truth has similar functions for spiritual warfare. With the belt of truth, one does not succumb to the onslaught of lies. As the Scripture clearly states, that liars have no part in God's Kingdom. Truth is very vital in spiritual warfare!

Breastplate of Righteousness:
This word breastplate conjures up the idea of a chest protector that one would wear into battle. It is associated with armour in the average person's mind. However, as I studied about the breastplate, there are some parallels that are amazing!

Breastplate comes from the Greek word thorax, which refers to a corselet. This breastplate or corselet was comprised of two parts, which was designed to protect the body on both sides, from the neck to the middle. In the Bible, the word breastplate is used metaphorically for God's Righteousness and just as a physical breastplate covers the weak spot of the soldier wearing it; the breastplate of righteousness covers our weak spots.

In mammals, the thorax is the region of the body formed by the sternum, the thoracic vertebrae and the ribs. It extends from the neck to the diaphragm, and does not include the upper limbs. The heart and the lungs reside in the thoracic cavity along with many blood vessels.

The throat and heart area are interconnected; one unites or strengthens the other. So righteousness is to protect the heart and the neck. In the natural, you might understand why the Breastplate of Righteousness protects the heart, but you might wonder what the neck has to do with it. It is amazing how it all relates to Scripture! Bear with me as we examine the Scriptures supporting this premise:

The Importance Of The Heart
There are over 875 passages of Scriptures on the heart in the Bible. Some of them can be found in: Psalms 15:2, Psalms 24:1-5, Psalms 51:17, Psalms 66:18, Proverbs 23:15-17, Jeremiah17:5-10, Matthew 5:8, Matthew 6:21, Matthew 15:8, 18-19, Romans 10:10, 1 Timothy 1:5, 2 Timothy 2:22, Hebrews 4:12

For purpose of this study, I would like for us to explore the following:

> "Dear friend, listen well to my words; tune your ears to my voice. (21) Keep my message in plain view at all times. Concentrate! Learn it by heart! (22) Those who discover these words live, really live; body and soul, they're bursting with health. (23) *Keep vigilant watch over your heart; that's where life starts.* (24) Don't talk out of both sides of your mouth; avoid careless banter, white lies, and gossip. (25) Keep your eyes straight ahead; ignore all sideshow distractions." [MSG Proverbs 4:20-25 Italics Added]

> "My son, pay attention to what I say; listen closely to my words. 21 Do not let them out of your sight, keep them within your heart; 22 for they are life to those who find them and health to a man's whole body. 23 *Above all else, guard your heart, for it is the wellspring of life.* 24 Put away perversity from your mouth; keep corrupt talk far from your lips. 25 Let your eyes look straight ahead, fix your gaze directly before you." [NIV]

From these two verses we see that the heart is the mission control centre, or the hub of everything we do. It is the command centre, which needs to be safeguarded.

To tie the neck into this whole anatomy lesson, and to determine why the neck needs protection as well, we read in the Bible that when someone is unrighteous or unrepentant, the Bible calls them "stiff-necked or proud" [Such as in Acts 7:51, Exodus 32:1-9, Deuteronomy 9:6-17].

We read more about it in:
"To the LORD your God belong the heavens, even the highest heavens, the earth and everything in it. 15 Yet the LORD set his affection on your forefathers and loved them, and he chose you, their descendants, above all the nations, as it is today. 16 *Circumcise your hearts, therefore, and do not be stiff-necked any longer.* 17 For the LORD your God is God of gods and Lord of lords, the great God, mighty and awesome, who shows no partiality and accepts no bribes."
[Deuteronomy 10:14-17 Italics Added]

God wants us to guard our hearts and to not be stiff-necked or proud. Only then can His Righteousness be appropriated through the Grace given to receive it.

Feet shod with the Gospel of Peace:
"And having shod your feet in preparation [to face the enemy with the firm-footed stability, the promptness, and the readiness produced by the good news] of the Gospel of peace." [AMP]

Footwear is a vital part of our lives as it protects our feet from damage. Without proper footwear, the feet are susceptible to conditions that affect the whole body. The feet are the pillars on which the entire body stands. As a matter of fact Apostle Paul when writing to the Corinthian church about the Gifts of the Spirit he said, "that the Head [Jesus Christ] cannot say to the feet that He has no need of them" [1 Corinthians 12:21].

The spiritual footwear that comes from the "Gospel of Peace" gives us the firm-footed stability, promptness and readiness we'll need to face our sprightly adversary. The term "Gospel of Peace" refers to the peace we have with God through Jesus Christ: "Therefore, since we have been justified through faith, we have peace with God through our Lord Jesus Christ, through whom we have gained access by faith into this grace in which we now stand. And we rejoice in the hope of the glory of God" [Romans 5:1-2].

The Shield of Faith:
The Greek word for faith in the above verses is *Pistis*, which means: Conviction of the truth of anything, belief; in the New Testament of a conviction or belief respecting man's relationship to God and divine things, generally with the included idea of trust and holy fervour born of faith and joined with it.

The following provides further insight on the meaning of faith:

> "Now faith is the substance of things hoped for, the evidence of things not seen. ...6 But without faith it is impossible to please Him, for he who comes to God must believe that He is, and that He is a rewarder of those who diligently seek Him." [Hebrews 11:1, 6]

Our faith must be based on the truth of the word of God where we trust that God will protect us from the evil one and we believe that through faith we have Jesus Christ's authority over evil powers. Any other source is neither reliable nor trustworthy. The devil's primary tactic against our faith is to persuade us to believe lies so that our faith is not founded on truth. Once we believe lies, our shield of faith is basically deactivated, giving the enemy access to our heart and lives.

The Helmet of Salvation:
Military helmets have been worn since ancient times and were primarily a defensive covering for the head but it was designed as armour to protect the head, face, and sometimes the neck from the cutting blows of swords, spears, arrows, and other weapons.

In the 18th and 19th centuries, with the growing effectiveness of firearms and the consequent decline in use of the sword and spear, helmets largely disappeared except for the use of light helmets by cavalry. However, this did not last for long as the steel helmet reappeared as a standard item for infantry during World War I because it protected the head against the high-velocity metal fragments of exploding artillery shells.

Today's militaries continue with their use of helmets for their soldiers in battle and the steel helmets of yesteryear have given way to high-quality helmets made of ballistic materials such as Kevlar, which have excellent bullet and fragmentation stopping power.

Just as in the natural the helmet protects the head, in the spiritual, the helmet protects our minds. The mind is the battleground of the enemy, thus a spiritual covering or protection is needed. The Bible declares that as man thinks so is he [Proverbs 23:7]. Since man's beginning, satan has focused his attacks on people's minds. satan cannot force us to sin, but rather he must persuade us to commit sin. The mind is the control centre, which decides if we will sin, or not. By persuading us to sin the devil expects that this will increase his demonic power and influence in the world.

Considering the strategic value of our minds, God has given us the helmet of salvation to protect us from the enemy. This helmet best functions by the Peace that comes from God, which is activated when our minds are focused on Him and trusting in Him.

> "Do not be anxious about anything, but in everything, by prayer and petition, with thanksgiving, present your requests to God. [7]And the peace of God, which transcends all understanding, will guard your hearts and your minds in Christ Jesus." [Philippians 4:6-7]

> "You will keep him in perfect peace, Whose mind is stayed on You, Because he trusts in You."

The helmet of salvation, like the other pieces of armour, is dependent on our faith in God and His promises.

The Sword of the Spirit:
The Sword of the Spirit is a powerful weapon of spiritual warfare. It is the only piece of our armour that is used for the offensive and it is very powerful indeed! The sword is formed by speaking God's Word.

As a matter of fact from the very beginning, God has spoken words that have powerfully influenced everything that exists. For example, God created the heavens and earth by speaking them into existence! The Bible says:

> "By faith we understand that the worlds were framed by the word of God, so that the things which are seen

were not made out of things which are visible". [Hebrews 11:3]

Since God created us in His likeness, we too have the ability to release power through speech. For example, our words can bring life and death [Proverbs 18:21]. They can build people up or tear them down [James Chapter 3]

We have come to the end of this chapter and in closing, the Scripture that I believe best puts this power of addressing the enemy, which will cause him to listen, is found in the following:

> "O LORD, our Lord, How excellent is Your name in all the earth, Who set Your glory above the heavens! 2 Out of the mouth of babes and nursing infants You have ordained strength, Because of Your enemies, That You may silence the enemy and the avenger." [Psalms 8:1-2]

Matthew presents to us the cosmic battle of all ages between Jesus and the enemy. Our Lord and Saviour and Commander in chief won the battle hands-down by applying the Sword of the Spirit, which is the Word of God:

> "Then Jesus was led by the Spirit into the desert to be tempted by the devil. 2 After fasting forty days and forty nights, he was hungry. 3 The tempter came to him and said, "If you are the Son of God, tell these stones to become bread." 4 Jesus answered, "It is written: `Man does not live on bread alone, but on every word that comes from the mouth of God.'" 5 Then the devil took him to the holy city and had him stand on the highest point of the temple. 6 "If you are the Son of God," he said, "throw yourself down. For it is written: "`He will command his angels concerning

you, and they will lift you up in their hands, so that you will not strike your foot against a stone.'" 7 Jesus answered him, "It is also written: `Do not put the Lord your God to the test.'" 8 Again, the devil took him to a very high mountain and showed him all the kingdoms of the world and their splendour. 9 "All this I will give you," he said, "if you will bow down and worship me." 10 Jesus said to him, "Away from me, Satan! For it is written: `Worship the Lord your God, and serve him only.'" 11 Then the devil left him, and angels came and attended him." [Matthew 4:1-11]

We the Church of Jesus Christ have been equipped and mandated to do the same!!! The ability for us to use the Sword of the Spirit, which is the Word of God, is not limited to mature, grown up Believers. It is available even to infants, because God has already ordained that out the mouth of babes and infants He has ordained strength to silence the enemy [Psalms 8:2]. So teach your children [and new converts] the Word of God! Let them speak into their situations from a tender age.

As I end this book allow me to leave you with the words of the 46th Psalms that was the inspiration for that great song [A Mighty Fortress Is Our God] of the ages penned by Martin Luther the Great Reformer!

> "God *is* our refuge and strength, A very present help in trouble. 2 Therefore we will not fear, Even though the earth be removed, And though the mountains be carried into the midst of the sea; 3 *Though* its waters roar *and* be troubled, *Though* the mountains shake with its swelling. Selah 4 *There is* a river whose streams shall make glad the city of God, The holy *place* of the tabernacle of the Most High. 5 God *is* in the midst

of her, she shall not be moved; God shall help her, just at the break of dawn. 6 The nations raged, the kingdoms were moved; He uttered His voice, the earth melted. 7 The LORD of hosts *is* with us; The God of Jacob *is* our refuge. Selah 8 Come, behold the works of the LORD, Who has made desolations in the earth. 9 He makes wars cease to the end of the earth; He breaks the bow and cuts the spear in two; He burns the chariot in the fire. 10 Be still, and know that I *am* God; I will be exalted among the nations, I will be exalted in the earth! 11 The LORD of hosts *is* with us; The God of Jacob *is* our refuge. Selah"

OTHER EXCITING TITLES
By Michael Scantlebury

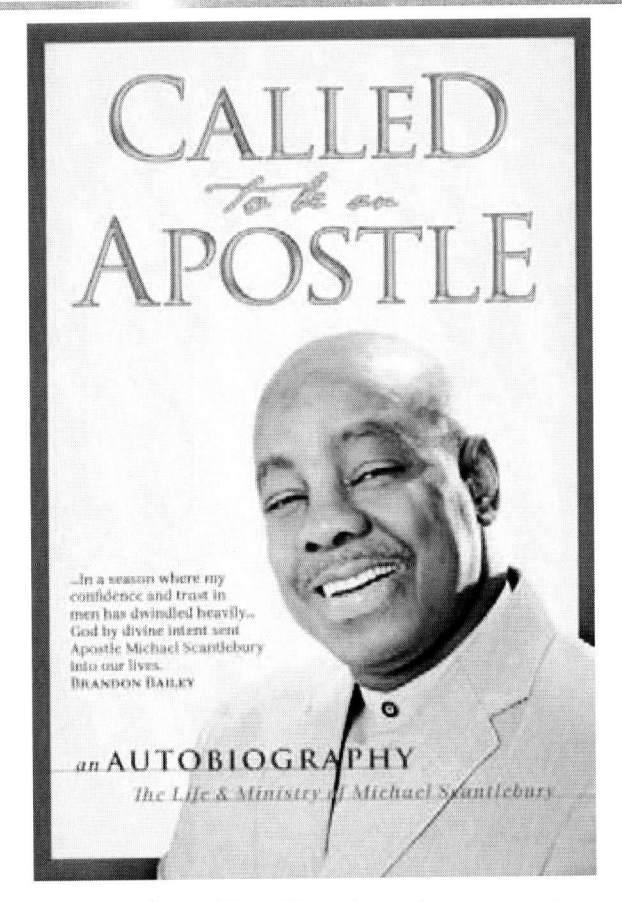

CALLED TO BE AN APOSTLE

This autobiography spans fifty-two years of my life on the earth thus far and I have the hope of living several more... Our home was always packed with young people and we did enjoy times of really wonderful fellowship! Although we were experiencing these wonderful times of fellowship my appetite and desire to grow in the things of God continued unabated. I continued to read anything and everything that I could put my hands on that would strengthen my life. I began reading Wigglesworth, Moody, Finney, Idahosa, Lake, and the list went on and on! But the more I read the more this question burned in my heart—*"why is it that every time we hear/read about a move of God, it is always miles away and in another country? Why can't I experience some of the things that I am reading about?"* Little did I know the Lord would answer that desire...

**For ordering details see the end of this book
Or visit www.wordalive.ca**

a refreshing new book by

MICHAEL SCANTLEBURY
foreword by Bishop Tudor Bismark

GOOD OR BAD

A little leaven leavens the whole lump

LEAVEN REVEALED

I believe this book seeks to regain some lost territory in our corporate mind as the Church, the Ekklesia in the principle of what we believe and live.
— BISHOP TUDOR BISMARK

LEAVEN REVEALED

The Bible has a lot to say about *leaven* and its effects upon the Believer. Leaven as an ingredient gives a false sense of growth. In the New Testament there are at least six types of *leaven* spoken about and we will be exploring them in detail, in order to ensure that our lives are completely free of the first five, and completely influenced by the sixth! These types of leaven include the following: The leaven of the Pharisees; The leaven of the Sadducees; The leaven of the Galatians; The leaven of Herod; The leaven of the Corinthians. However, the Leaven of the Kingdom of God, is the only type of leaven that has the power and capacity to bring about true growth and lasting change to our lives.

**For ordering details see the end of this book
Or visit www.wordalive.ca**

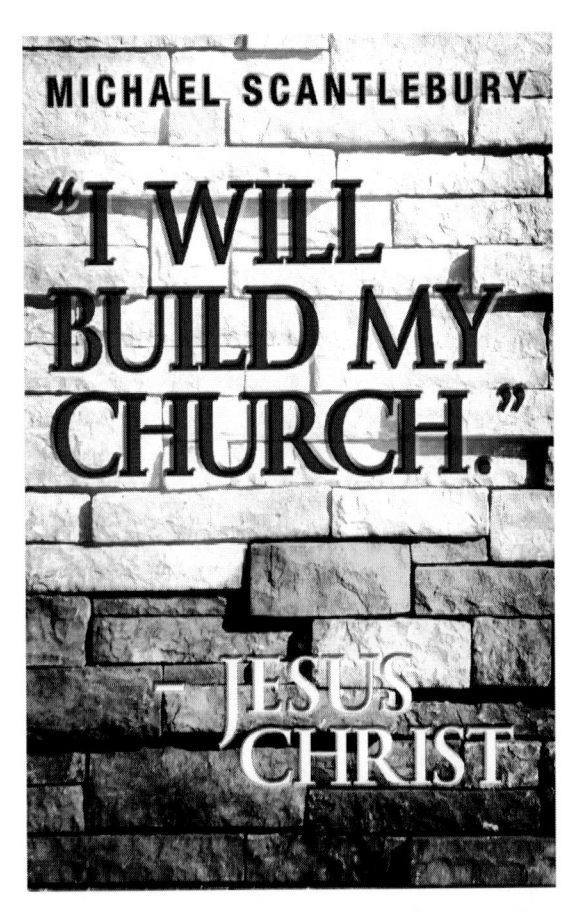

I Will Build My Church. – Jesus Christ

> "For we are his *masterpiece*, created in Christ Jesus for good works that God prepared long ago to be our way of life."
> Ephesians 2:10

What a powerful picture of the Church of Jesus Christ—His Masterpiece! Reference to a *masterpiece* lends to the idea that there are other pieces and among them all, this particular one stands head and shoulders above the rest! This is so true when it comes to the Church that Jesus Christ is building; when you place it alongside everything else that God has created, The Church is by far His Masterpiece!

**For ordering details see the end of this book
Or visit www.wordalive.ca**

JESUS CHRIST THE APOSTLE AND HIGH PRIEST

There is a dimension to the apostolic nature of Jesus Christ that I would like to capture in His one-on-one encounters with several people during the time He walked the face of the earth and functioned as Apostle. In this book we will explore several significant encounters that Jesus Christ had with different people where valuable principles and insight can be gleaned. They are designed to change your life!

**For ordering details see the end of this book
Or visit www.wordalive.ca**

FIVE PILLARS OF THE APOSTOLIC

It has become very evident that a new day has dawned in the earth, as the Lord restores the foundational ministry of the Apostle back to His Church. This book will give you a clear and concise understanding of what the Holy Spirit is doing in The Church today!

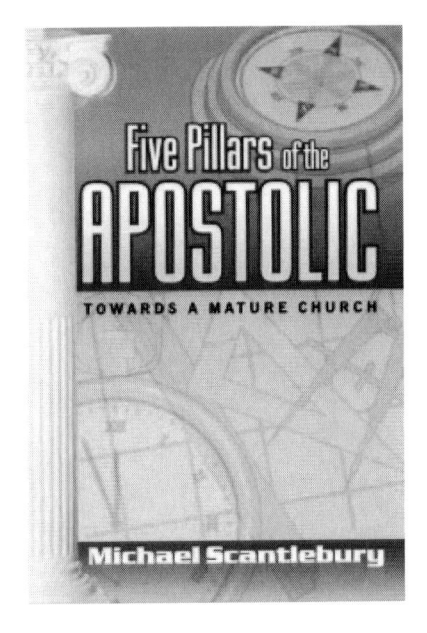

APOSTOLIC PURITY

In every dispensation, in every move of God's Holy Spirit to bring restoration and reformation to His Church, righteousness, holiness and purity has always been of utmost importance to the Lord. This book will challenge your to walk pure as you seek to fulfill God's Will for your life and ministry!

For ordering details see the end of this book
Or visit www.wordalive.ca

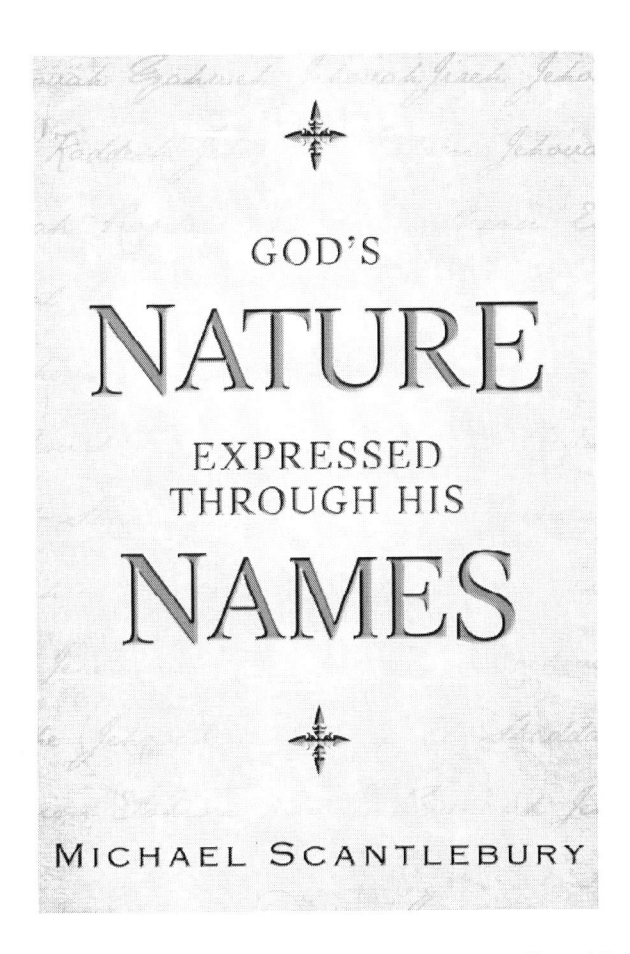

God's Nature Expressed Through His Names

How awesome it would be when we encounter God's Nature through the varied expressions of His Names. His Names give us reference and guidance as to how He works towards and in us as His people—and by extension to society! As a matter of fact it adds a while new meaning to how you draw near to Him; and by this you can now begin to know His Ways because you have come into relationship with His Nature!

> For ordering details see the end of this book
> Or visit www.wordalive.ca

INTERNAL REFORMATION

"Internal Reformation" is multifaceted. It is an ecclesiology laying out the blue print of the Church Jesus Christ is building in today's world. At the same time it is a manual laying out the modus operandi of how Believers are called to function as dynamic, militant overcomers who are powerful because they carry internally the very character and DNA of Jesus Christ.

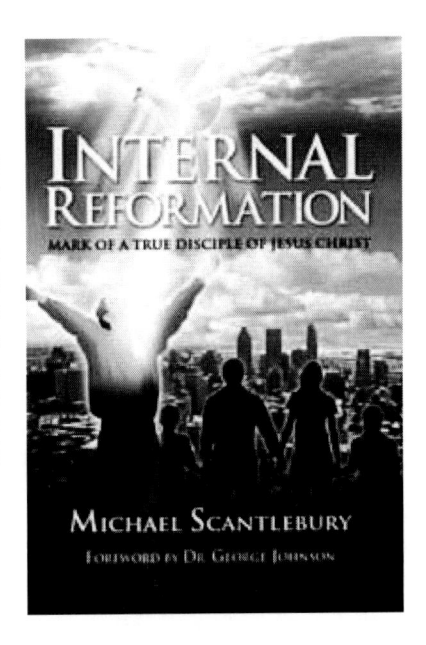

KINGDOM ADVANCING PRAYER VOLUME I

The Church of Jesus Christ is stronger and much more determined and equipped than she has ever been, and strong, aggressive, powerful, Spirit-Filled, Kingdom-centred prayers are being lifted in every nation in the earth. This kind of prayer is released from the heart of Father God into the hearts of His people, as we seek for His Glory to cover the earth as the waters cover the sea.

**For ordering details see the end of this book
Or visit www.wordalive.ca**

APOSTOLIC REFORMATION

If the axe is dull, And one does not sharpen the edge, Then he must use more strength; But wisdom brings success." (Ecclesiastes 10:10) For centuries the Church of Jesus Christ has been using quite a bit of strength while working with a dull axe (sword, Word of God, revelation), in trying to get the job done. This has been largely due to the fact that she has been functioning without Apostles, the ones who have been graced and anointed by the Lord, with the ability to sharpen.

**For ordering details see the end of this book
Or visit www.wordalive.ca**

KINGDOM ADVANCING PRAYER VOLUME II

Prayer is calling for the Bridegroom's return, and for the Bride to be made ready. Prayers are storming the heavens and binding the "strong men" declaring and decreeing God's Kingdom rule in every jurisdiction. This is what we call Kingdom Advancing Prayer. What a *Glorious Day* to be *Alive* and to be in the *Will* and *Plan of Father God*! *Hallelujah*!

KINGDOM ADVANCING PRAYER VOLUME III

One of the keys to the amazing rise to greater functionality of the Church is the clear understanding of what we call Kingdom Advancing Prayer. This kind of prayer reaches into the very core of the demonic stronghold and destroys demonic kings and princes and establishes the Kingdom and Purpose of the Lord. This is the kind of prayer that Jesus Christ engaged in, to bring to pass the will of His Father while He was upon planet earth.

**For ordering details see the end of this book
Or visit www.wordalive.ca**

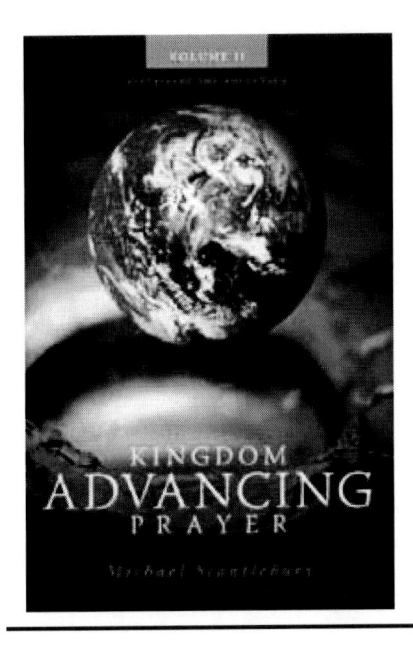

IDENTIFYING AND DEFEATING THE JEZEBEL SPIRIT

I declare to you with the greatest of conviction that we are living in the days when Malachi 4:5-6 is being fulfilled. Elijah in his day had to confront and deal with a false spiritual order and government that was established and set up by an evil woman called Jezebel and her spineless husband called Ahab. This spirit is still active in the earth and in the Church; however the Lord is restoring His holy apostles and prophets to identify and destroy this spirit as recorded in Revelation 2:18-23!

ORDER FROM
PRESENT TRUTH MEDIA
Orders please call 604-599-3542 | Fax 604-599-3543
Website – https://present-truthpublishing.com
Website – www.dominion-life.org

Ordering Information

Book Orders Please Contact:

Word Alive Press

In Canada/USA:
Phone: 866.967.3782 | Fax: 800.352.9272
International: Phone: 204.667.1400 | Fax: 204.669.0947
Website – www.wordalive.ca

Or From:
Present Truth Media

Phone: 604.599.3542 | Fax: 604.599.3543
Website – https://present-truthpublishing.com

Also Available From:
www.amazon.ca/com
www.chapters.Indigo.ca
www.barnesandnoble.com